Mykonos Travel Guide 2023

"Your Definitive Handbook to Unveil the Enchantment of Mykonos in 2023"

James S. Abbott

All rights reserved. No part of this publication may be reproduced, distributed, or transmitted in any form or by any means, including photocopying, recording, or other electronic or mechanical methods, without the prior written permission of the publisher, except in the case of brief quotations embodied in critical reviews and certain other noncommercial uses permitted by copyright law.

Copyright © James S. Abbott, 2023.

Table of content

Table of content	3
Introduction	6
Chapter 1	**9**
Your Essential Mykonos Travel Companion	9
Navigating Travel Logistics in 2023	9
Arrival and Transportation Tips	15
Weather Insights for Your Visit	25
Packing Essentials for Island Life	30
Staying Safe and Healthy	40
Staying Connected: Internet and Communication	45
Chapter 2	**50**
Embracing Enchanting Mykonos Town	50
Chora's Mesmerizing White-Washed Beauty	**50**
Windmills and Panoramic Views	59
Exploring Little Venice's Bohemian Charm	68
Icons Unveiled: Landmarks and Art Galleries	75
Sunset Delights at Alefkandra Square	86
Chapter 3	**92**
Beaches of Mykonos: Sun, Sea, and Serenity	92
Psarou Beach: Luxury and Glamour	92
Paradise Beach: Vibrant Parties and Clear Waters	98
Super Paradise Beach: Entertainment and Celeb Sightings	

104
    Elia Beach: Tranquil Escape and Crystal Sands   110
    Agios Sostis: Secluded Bliss and Natural Beauty   116

Chapter 4   **122**
    Mykonos Beyond the Shorelines   122
    Unearth Delos Island's Ancient Secrets   122
    Ano Mera - Immerse in Traditional Village Life   127
    Sunset at Armenistis Lighthouse   134
    Unraveling the Mystique of Ftelia Archaeological Site 143
    Horseback Riding and Rural Escapes   148

Chapter 5   **153**
    Crafting Unforgettable 2023 Experiences   153
    Mykonos Nightlife - Epic Parties and Entertainment   153
    Yachting and Sailing: Aegean Dreams Set Sail   159
    Culinary Journeys: Greek Delights and Gourmet Feasts 165
    Mykonos Shopping: A Fusion of Tradition and Modernity 175
    Retreat to Wellness: Spa Escapes and Rejuvenation   183

Chapter 6:   **189**
    Celebrate Summer in Mykonos   189
    Mykonos' Cultural Feast: Festivals and Events   189
    Musical Harmony: Mykonos' Music and Arts Festivals 210
    Beach Parties and DJ Sets   217
    Vibrant 2023 - A Year of Mykonos Celebrations   229

Chapter 7   **236**
    Unveiling the Best of Your Mykonos Journey   236
    Accommodation Excellence: Your Perfect Retreat   236

Mykonos on Wheels: Transportation Wisdom	251
Cultural Etiquette and Responsible Tourism	256
Capturing Memories: Photography Hotspots	264
Conversing with Locals: Essential Greek Phrases	276
Conclusion	**283**

Introduction

Welcome to the alluring island of Mykonos, where the calm, blue seas of the Aegean Sea meet the lively vitality of Mediterranean culture. We invite you to explore the breathtaking beauty, rich culture, and magnetic attraction of Mykonos in the extraordinary year of 2023 by reading our travel guide. You're about to go off on a voyage that promises unique experiences and endless discovery as the sun spreads its golden glow over the island's stunning beaches and historic towns.

Mykonos, a gem in the Cyclades archipelago of Greece, has long been praised for its magnificent scenery, whitewashed structures, and vibrant nightlife. The island greets in 2023 with a fresh enthusiasm, providing a variety of experiences to suit every traveler's preferences. Mykonos has something extraordinary in store for you, whether you're searching for tranquility on gorgeous coasts, cultural insights into old civilizations, or to fully immerse yourself in the rhythm of exuberant festivals.

Prepare to be taken to a world where ancient history and modern luxury coexist, where the excitement of exploration combines with the friendliness of the locals. As you click through these pages. To make sure that your trip through Mykonos is nothing less than wonderful, we carefully selected this guide. This book is your key to unlocking Mykonos in all its splendor, from the ideal times to visit to find hidden treasures, from indulging in delicious cuisine to capturing the island's spirit via your lens.

Mykonos in 2023 therefore promises to surpass your expectations, regardless of whether you're a sun seeker, a history enthusiast, a partygoer, or just a visitor thirsty for new experiences. Mykonos is eager to reveal its mysteries and enchantments to you, so pack your curiosity, excitement, and spirit of adventure. Your arrival will be greeted by the clear seas, the cobblestone streets, and the colorful sunsets. Together, let's set out on this voyage to discover Mykonos' seductive appeal in 2023.

Chapter 1

Your Essential Mykonos Travel Companion

Navigating Travel Logistics in 2023

Mykonos is a bright tapestry where the warm Greek friendliness meets the crystal blue of the Aegean Sea. Traveling to this enchanted island paradise requires careful planning. To make sure that your landing on the coasts of Mykonos is flawless and that your discovery of its treasures is nothing short of extraordinary, this section reveals the intricate details of mastering travel logistics.

1. The Allure of Mykonos in 2023:
In 2023, Mykonos will continue to entice visitors from all over the world with the promise of exciting new experiences. This year is set to be memorable for Mykonos because of the island's recognizable white-washed architecture,

blue seas, and legendary nightlife. Whether you're a history enthusiast eager to learn about the island's fascinating past or a sun worshipper eager to enjoy its sun-drenched beaches, 2023 provides a blank slate for making priceless memories.

2. Arriving in Mykonos: Transportation Insights:
Selecting the best means of transportation is the first step in your trip to Mykonos. The island's entry point, Mykonos International Airport, accepts both domestic and international aircraft, making it a convenient option for visitors coming by air. Consider booking your flights well in advance to get preferred schedules and reasonable costs, especially during the busiest travel times, to guarantee a smooth and stress-free arrival.

3. Air Travel: Tips for Landing Smoothly:
When arriving in Mykonos via plane, the experience is filled with wonder and expectation. The busy environment at Mykonos International

Airport is evidence of how well-liked the island is, especially during the busiest travel seasons. Booking your flights well in advance is advised to guarantee a convenient and on-time arrival. Through careful planning, you may not only ensure availability but also book more convenient flight schedules that fit your schedule.

4. Sea Routes: Embarking on a Nautical Adventure:

The maritime route to Mykonos provides an alluring option for those looking for a more picturesque and slower arrival. Mykonos is connected to mainland Greece and other islands by ferries and catamarans, weaving a nautical web across the Aegean. Plan your ferry routes, timings, and ticket purchases to make the most of your maritime travel. Each boat voyage you the chance to take in the splendor of the Aegean landscape and prepares you for your Mykonos experience.

5. Private Yachts and Cruises: Experiencing Luxury:

Luxury visitors are also lured to Mykonos by its attractiveness due to the island's superb offers. You may approach the shores of Mykonos in a way that is consistent with its elegance by using private boat charters and cruise choices, which provide a taste of richness. It is possible to arrive in style while enjoying an uninterrupted view of the island's coastline magnificence by yachting through the Aegean Sea. For a spectacular arrival to Mykonos, take into account these opulent possibilities.

6. Local Transport: Getting Around Mykonos:

Once you get to Mykonos, a network of local transportation alternatives is ready to take you where you need to go. There are several ways to travel, including taxis, buses, and rental automobiles. Taxis provide easy point-to-point transportation that is great for short journeys. The bus system on the island, a practical option, connects important locations, enabling you to travel between locations at a reasonable price.

Consider hiring a car if you want the freedom to explore Mykonos on your schedule and are eager to do so. However, it is highly advised to make reservations in advance, particularly during the busy summer season.

7. Mykonos Welcomes You: Preparing for Your Adventure:
Planning meticulously is essential when you depart for Mykonos in 2023. Organizing your travel arrangements well in advance makes sure that everything goes well and without worry. Learn about the various modes of transportation on the island so you can easily transition from your arrival location to your selected location. Local organizations and tour operators are on hand to meet your requirements should you want support or tailored information. Strategic planning at the outset of your visit creates the conditions for a magical experience with Mykonos' allure.

8. Setting the Course for Your Mykonos Adventure:

The meticulous planning of your travel arrangements forms the prelude to an astonishing symphony of sensations as you enter the domain of Mykonos in 2023. The prologue of your island vacation is determined by your decision between the anticipation of air travel, the picturesque attraction of marine routes, and the elegance of luxury vessels. Make use of the chances provided by the several local transportation methods, each of which offers a unique perspective from which to examine Mykonos' many characteristics. You are prepared to embrace the appeal of 2023, a year brimming with possibilities for exploration and enchantment, as you finally step foot on Mykonos' shoreline. Your voyage has started, and the island's delights are waiting for you.

Arrival and Transportation Tips

Welcome to Mykonos' dynamic universe! Understanding the ins and outs of arrival and transportation before you set out on your journey to this alluring Greek island is crucial for ensuring a seamless and delightful visit. We'll explore the essential elements of traveling to Mykonos and navigating the island with ease in this part.

Arrival to Mykonos: Gateway to Aegean Magic

1. Flights to Mykonos: Connecting the World
By flight, Mykonos is simple to reach because of its excellent connections to significant cities throughout Europe and beyond. Your entryway to an Aegean paradise is Mykonos Airport (IATA: JMK), the island's international airport. Modern airport improvements provide speedy and comfortable travel for passengers. The number of flight alternatives dramatically

expands throughout the summer to handle the surge of tourists.

2. Navigating the Arrival Process

You'll be met by the pleasant Aegean wind and the anticipation of reaching Mykonos as you get off your plane. Your initial actions will guide you through the immigration and customs processes associated with your arrival. Make sure you have your passport, any applicable visas, and any relevant health disclosures ready before you go. Learn about Greece's admission regulations to ensure a smooth and stress-free experience.

3. Airport to Accommodation: Transfers

After you've completed the arrival procedures, it's time to make your way to your chosen accommodation. Mykonos Airport provides various transportation options just outside its doors. Taxis, shuttle services, and private transfers are readily available. Pre-arranging your transfer ensures a swift transition from the airport to your chosen lodgings, allowing you to begin your Mykonos experience without delay.

Getting Around Mykonos: Island Exploration Made Easy

1. Public Transportation: Buses and Beyond
A well-maintained and reasonably priced public bus system connects the main towns, sights, and beaches of Mykonos. The air-conditioned, contemporary buses provide passengers an opportunity to see local culture firsthand. Although bus crowding might occur during the busiest tourist seasons, schedules are often dependable. Make transport arrangements in advance and take in the stunning views of the island from the convenience of a bus seat.

2. Renting a Vehicle: Exploring at Your Pace
Renting a car is a great choice for individuals who want the most flexibility and freedom to travel off the main path. Rental companies provide a variety of options, including automobiles, scooters, and ATVs. Before

embarking on your independent adventures, make sure your driver's license is up to date and familiarize yourself with Greek traffic laws. Renting a car enables you to explore the island at your own pace while taking in breathtaking vistas.

3. Taxis and Ridesharing

In Mykonos, taxis are widely accessible and a reliable form of transportation, particularly if you want door-to-door service. Taxis are practical, but they may also be more expensive than alternative options. Mykonos is seeing the emergence of ridesharing services, which provide a contemporary touch to the island's transportation. However, since availability varies, it's a good idea to double-check before depending on ridesharing services.

4. Walking and Biking: Embracing the Charm

Mykonos is a pedestrian-friendly location that is ideal for strolls and bike journeys due to its small size. You are invited to explore on foot by the island's winding alleyways, which are lined with whitewashed structures and colorful bougainvillea. Bicycle rentals are widely available at lodgings, offering guests an eco-friendly and fun way to explore the neighborhood. By exploring Mykonos on foot or by bicycle, you may get a close-up view of its allure and beauty.

Navigating Mykonos: Tips and Insights

Local Etiquette and Customs:
As you revel in the beauty of Mykonos, it's important to respect the local customs and etiquette. When visiting churches, monasteries, or religious sites, dressing modestly is crucial as a sign of respect. Always ask for permission before photographing locals, as this gesture demonstrates your appreciation for their culture and privacy.

Embrace the Island's Energy:
Mykonos is renowned for its vibrant and lively atmosphere, particularly during the summer months. Engage in the island's spirited

celebrations, beach parties, and nightlife to fully immerse yourself in the local energy. Joining the festivities not only provides an opportunity to create unforgettable memories but also offers insights into the island's culture and zest for life.

Sustainable Tourism Practices:
In line with responsible travel, adopting sustainable practices during your Mykonos adventure is encouraged. Preserving the natural beauty of the island is a collective responsibility. Avoid littering, opt for reusable items, and support local businesses that prioritize sustainability. By making conscious choices, you contribute to safeguarding Mykonos' allure for future generations of travelers.

Staying Connected: Internet and Communication

Staying connected while exploring Mykonos is both convenient and straightforward. Most accommodations provide Wi-Fi access, enabling you to remain in touch with loved ones and share your experiences in real time. For those seeking seamless internet connectivity while on the go, consider purchasing a local SIM card. These cards offer data plans that allow you to access the internet and navigate the island with ease.

Airport Services and Amenities:
Mykonos Airport offers an array of services and amenities to ensure your arrival and departure are comfortable and enjoyable. Duty-free shopping allows you to indulge in a bit of retail therapy, offering a selection of local products and international brands. Cafes and eateries provide a range of options, from grabbing a quick snack to savoring a leisurely meal. Lounges offer a tranquil space where you can relax before or after your flight, making your airport experience a pleasant part of your journey.

Exploring Nearby Islands:
While Mykonos itself offers an abundance of attractions, consider embarking on day trips to neighboring islands. The island's strategic location in the Cyclades archipelago makes it an

ideal starting point for island-hopping adventures. Delos, a nearby UNESCO World Heritage Site, offers an opportunity to delve into ancient history. Paros, Naxos, and Santorini are among the neighboring islands accessible by ferry. Research ferry schedules and plan your visits to these enchanting destinations to enrich your Greek island experience.

Booking Tours and Activities:
To optimize your time in Mykonos and make the most of your visit, consider booking tours and activities in advance. Whether you're interested in historical tours, water sports, cultural excursions, or culinary experiences, there's a wide array of options to suit every traveler's interests. Online platforms and local tour operators offer comprehensive selections that cater to various preferences. Booking in advance ensures availability and allows you to seamlessly integrate these experiences into your itinerary.

Embrace Spontaneity:

While planning is important, leaving room for spontaneity can lead to some of the most cherished travel memories. While exploring Mykonos, seize opportunities to wander through charming streets, discover hidden cafes, and interact with friendly locals. Serendipitous encounters often provide unique insights into local life and can lead to unexpected and delightful experiences that enrich your journey.

Discovering Mykonos' transportation choices and navigating your arrival there are the first steps in discovering all of this enchanted island's delights. You may choose how you want to travel, from using public transportation to renting a car and more, so you can customize your trip to your needs. Understanding regional traditions, appreciating the island's vibrancy, and adopting eco-friendly decisions not only improve your trip but also help keep Mykonos alluring for future generations. The next sections of this travel book will describe the magic of Mykonos Town, the attractiveness of its sun-kissed beaches, and the riches that lay beyond the shorelines as you get ready to explore the island's charm further. Your adventure has just begun—immerse yourself in the magic that Mykonos.

Weather Insights for Your Visit

Travelers may find a year-round sanctuary on the island of Mykonos, known for its breathtaking scenery and allure of the Mediterranean. The weather on the island, an important consideration when making travel plans, adds to the overall enjoyment. This section delves into the intricacies of the climate on Mykonos and how it affects your vacation, enabling you to make well-informed choices about when to go and what to bring.

Understanding Mykonos' Climate:
Mykonos enjoys a classic Mediterranean climate, shaped by its proximity to the Aegean Sea. This results in mild, damp winters and hot, dry summers. Four distinct seasons guide the island's weather patterns:

1. Spring (March-May): Spring paints Mykonos with a canvas of blooming flora and rejuvenated landscapes. The temperatures climb gradually, ranging from 15°C (59°F) to 20°C (68°F),

making it an ideal time for exploring the island's charms without the scorching summer sun. This season bridges the tranquil winter and the vibrant summer, offering a blend of pleasant weather and fewer crowds.

2. Summer (June - August): The Mykonos summer is synonymous with liveliness, beach days, and exuberant nightlife. Average temperatures range from 25°C (77°F) to 30°C (86°F), with July and August occasionally reaching higher peaks. The island comes alive with bustling energy, parties, and an array of water-based activities, making it a favorite among sun-seekers and party enthusiasts.

3. Autumn (September - November): As summer fades, autumn introduces a milder pace to the island. With temperatures ranging from 20°C (68°F) to 25°C (77°F) in September, gradually cooling down in the following months, this season offers a more tranquil atmosphere. The beaches are less crowded, and the weather

remains inviting for exploring the town's alleys or indulging in outdoor adventures.

4. Winter (December - February): While winter sees a decrease in tourist activity, Mykonos still carries its unique charm. Rainfall increases and temperatures hover between 10°C (50°F) to 15°C (59°F). This season is ideal for those seeking solitude, peaceful strolls by the sea, and a more intimate connection with the local culture.

Pack Smart for Mykonos

Your choice of clothing can significantly enhance your experience on the island:

- Summer Essentials: If you're drawn to Mykonos during the summer, pack light, breathable attire such as shorts, sundresses, and swimsuits. Shield yourself from the sun with sunscreen, a wide-brimmed hat, and sunglasses.

- Spring and Autumn Attire: These transitional seasons require versatile clothing options. Pack a mix of short-sleeved shirts, lightweight jackets or sweaters, and comfortable pants. Be prepared for the occasional rain shower by including an umbrella or rain jacket.

- Warmth for Winter: If you're exploring Mykonos during the winter, prioritize warmth. Pack cozy sweaters, long pants, and a waterproof jacket. Sturdy yet comfortable walking shoes are essential for navigating the town's charming cobbled streets.

Rainfall and Precipitation

While Mykonos is known for its sunshine, it's worth noting that winter ushers in more frequent rain showers. November typically receives the highest amount of rainfall. When visiting during this period, having waterproof gear and suitable footwear ensures you're prepared for any weather conditions.

Tailoring Activities to the Weather:
Your chosen activities can be enriched by understanding Mykonos' weather. The calm

waters of summer are perfect for water sports and beach relaxation. Spring and autumn provide excellent conditions for exploring historical sites and indulging in outdoor adventures. In winter, enjoy quieter walks through town and take advantage of the island's culinary delights.

Final Thoughts:
By aligning your travel plans with Mykonos' climate, you're poised to create a well-rounded and fulfilling experience. The island's diverse seasons offer something for every traveler, whether you seek vibrant summer festivities, peaceful springtime charm, or cozy winter seclusion. Your Mykonos journey, guided by a deep understanding of its weather nuances, promises to be an unforgettable exploration of this Mediterranean gem.

Packing Essentials for Island Life

Mykonos awaits you with bright days, peaceful beaches, and exciting evenings. The key to making the most of your island excursion is to pack wisely. Here is a complete list of everything you need to be ready for every aspect of Mykonos' allure in 2023.

1. Lightweight Clothing for Sunny Days:
Mykonos' climate is characterized by sunshine and warmth, especially during the peak summer months. Pack an array of lightweight and breathable clothing to stay comfortable and stylish as you explore the island. Choose natural fabrics like cotton and linen that allow your skin to breathe, and opt for light colors to reflect the sun's rays. Include items such as flowy dresses, shorts, skirts, and airy tops to keep you cool and effortlessly chic.

2. Beachwear and Swimwear:
With Mykonos boasting some of the most beautiful beaches in the world, swimwear is a non-negotiable. Pack a variety of swimwear options, from classic bikinis to stylish one-pieces. Consider designs that suit your style and offer comfort for hours of beach lounging. Don't forget to include a chic cover-up that can seamlessly transition from beach to cafe, a wide-brimmed hat for sun protection, and comfortable flip-flops for easy sandy strolls.

3. Comfortable Footwear:
The essence of Mykonos lies in exploration, from meandering through the charming streets of Chora to wandering off the beaten path. Make sure your feet are ready for the journey by packing a variety of comfortable footwear. Alongside your stylish sandals and espadrilles, include a pair of well-cushioned walking shoes. A versatile set of sneakers or trainers is essential if you're planning on venturing into the island's captivating hiking trails.

4. Stylish Evening Attire:

While Mykonos is a paradise during the day, its nights are equally enchanting. The island's bustling nightlife and upscale restaurants call for stylish evening attire. Pack a selection of elegant outfits that capture the island's chic spirit. Consider bringing a sundress for beachfront dinners, smart-casual separates that effortlessly transition from day to night or a well-fitted linen shirt paired with lightweight trousers.

5. Sun Protection:

With endless sunny days ahead, protecting your skin from the sun's rays is paramount. Pack a high-SPF sunscreen to shield your skin from harmful UV rays. Don't forget to include a pair of quality sunglasses that offer proper UV protection. A wide-brimmed hat serves a dual purpose by keeping you shaded and adding a touch of glamor to your island look. If you're prone to sunburns, consider bringing along a travel-sized bottle of aloe vera gel to soothe your skin after sun exposure.

6. Travel-Friendly Toiletries:
Streamline your toiletry bag by opting for travel-sized essentials. This includes shampoo, conditioner, body wash, and moisturizer. Mykonos' relaxed vibe makes it an ideal place to embrace a more natural look, so pack minimal makeup and skincare products. Be sure to include good quality and high SPF lip balm to protect your lips from the sun and keep them moisturized.

7. Light Layers for Cooler Evenings:
Evenings in Mykonos, while warm, can sometimes bring a slight chill in the air. Pack a light cardigan or a stylish jacket to layer over your outfits when the sun goes down. This ensures you're comfortable as you enjoy a stroll along the coastline or a romantic dinner by the sea.

8. Daypack or Beach Bag:
An essential companion for your daytime excursions, a practical yet stylish daypack or beach bag is a must. Choose a design that can

accommodate your essentials, including sunscreen, water bottle, camera, guidebook, and personal items. This ensures your hands are free to capture photos, explore markets, or simply soak in the island's beauty.

9. Universal Adapter and Chargers:
To stay connected and keep your devices charged throughout your Mykonos adventure, pack a universal adapter that works with the local power outlets. Ensure your phone, camera, and other gadgets are always ready to capture the island's breathtaking scenery and your cherished moments.

10. Travel Documents and Essentials:
The foundation of any successful journey is having your travel documents in order. Ensure you have your passport, flight tickets, travel insurance policy, and any necessary visas. Organize these documents in a secure travel wallet or pouch to keep them safe and easily accessible throughout your trip.

11. Travel-Friendly Accessories:

Accessorizing is the perfect way to infuse your style into your island wardrobe. Pack a variety of versatile accessories to elevate your outfits and enhance your overall look. A lightweight scarf can add a pop of color or serve as a cover-up when needed. Statement jewelry, such as bold earrings or a chunky necklace, can effortlessly transform a simple outfit into a fashion statement. Don't forget to include a foldable hat that not only shields you from the sun but also adds a touch of sophistication to your beachy ensembles.

12. Reusable Water Bottle:

Staying hydrated is paramount, especially in Mykonos' sun-soaked climate. Packing a reusable water bottle not only helps you reduce plastic waste but also ensures you have access to water wherever you go. Refill it throughout the day to stay refreshed during your explorations and beach outings.

13. Lightweight Daywear Bag:
For your daytime adventures, opt for a lightweight crossbody bag or a backpack that combines functionality with style. This bag will be your constant companion as you venture through Chora's narrow alleys or along the island's scenic trails. Look for a design with multiple compartments to keep your essentials organized and easily accessible.

14. First Aid Kit and Medications:
Safety and health should always be a priority when traveling. Pack a basic first aid kit containing essentials such as adhesive bandages, antiseptic wipes, pain relievers, and any necessary prescription medications. By having these items on hand, you'll be prepared to address minor injuries or health concerns that may arise during your journey.

15. Travel Journal and Essentials:
Immersing yourself in Mykonos' beauty and culture is an experience worth capturing. Bring along a travel journal to jot down your thoughts,

observations, and memorable moments. Consider including a high-quality pen and a small pouch to store mementos like postcards, ticket stubs, or even small seashells as tangible reminders of your journey.

16. Entertainment and Reading Material:
In moments of relaxation, having entertainment options is essential. Pack a captivating novel, a travel guidebook, or your favorite e-reader to indulge in during beach lounging or downtime. Not only does this provide entertainment, but it also allows you to fully immerse yourself in the island's ambiance.

17. Cash and Currency:
While credit cards are widely accepted, having some local currency can be advantageous, especially in smaller establishments or for tipping. Inform your bank about your travel plans to ensure your cards are usable abroad, and carry a mix of cash denominations to cover various expenses.

18. Travel Insurance and Important Contacts:
Having copies of your travel insurance details and emergency contact numbers readily available is crucial. Store these documents in a separate pouch or section of your luggage for quick access in case of unforeseen circumstances.

19. Laundry Solutions:
For longer stays or if you prefer to pack light, consider including a small supply of travel-sized laundry detergent or laundry sheets. This allows you to refresh your clothing during your trip, ensuring you always have clean and comfortable options to wear.

20. Flexibility and Mindset:
While packing essentials is essential, remember that a flexible mindset is equally valuable. Mykonos invites you to embrace its relaxed pace and spontaneous moments. Be open to unexpected experiences, interactions with locals, and the chance to create memories beyond your initial plans.

By thoughtfully packing these essentials, you're not just preparing for a journey to Mykonos; you're equipping yourself with an immersive experience that encapsulates the island's charm, style, and spirit. Your suitcase isn't just holding items—it's holding the promise of adventure, discovery, and unforgettable moments that await you on this captivating island in 2023.

Staying Safe and Healthy

Taking precautions to ensure your safety and well-being is essential when traveling to Mykonos in 2023. Taking proactive measures to be safe and healthy will improve your experience and enable you to make the most of your voyage as you take in the island's beauty and dynamic environment.

1. Understanding Local Laws and Regulations:
Before you immerse yourself in Mykonos' charms, familiarize yourself with the local laws and regulations. While Mykonos is generally considered safe, respecting local customs, traditions, and rules is essential. Familiarize yourself with guidelines related to photography, beach etiquette, and behavior in public spaces.

2. Health Precautions and Medical Facilities:
Prioritize your well-being by staying informed about health precautions. Ensure you have comprehensive travel insurance that covers medical emergencies. If you require prescription

medications, bring an ample supply and carry a copy of your prescription. Mykonos has medical facilities equipped to handle minor medical issues, but for more serious concerns, nearby islands like Naxos and Paros offer larger medical centers.

3. Sun Safety and Hydration:
The Aegean sun can be intense, even in 2023. Protect yourself by wearing sunscreen with a high SPF, sunglasses, a hat, and lightweight clothing that covers your skin. Stay hydrated throughout the day, especially if you're spending time on the beaches or exploring under the sun. Carry a refillable water bottle and refill it frequently to beat the heat.

4. Responsible Alcohol Consumption:
Mykonos' vibrant nightlife scene is a major draw, but it's crucial to practice responsible alcohol consumption. Be mindful of your limits and never leave your drink unattended. Stay hydrated between alcoholic beverages and always have a designated driver or transportation

arranged if you plan to enjoy the island's nightlife.

5. Food and Water Safety:
Savoring local cuisine is an integral part of any travel experience, and Mykonos offers a plethora of culinary delights. To ensure food safety, dine at reputable establishments and opt for cooked meals. While the tap water in Mykonos is generally safe for brushing your teeth, it's advisable to drink bottled water to prevent any potential stomach discomfort.

6. Wildlife and Nature Interaction:
Mykonos is home to various species of wildlife, including birds and marine life. While interacting with nature is a wonderful aspect of the island, it's crucial to maintain a respectful distance and not disturb the animals or their habitats. If you're lucky enough to spot sea turtles or other wildlife while snorkeling or swimming, admire them from a distance to preserve their natural behavior.

7. Emergency Contacts and Safety Measures:
As a responsible traveler, it's wise to have a list of emergency contacts on hand. This should include local authorities, the nearest embassy or consulate, and the contact information of your accommodation. Familiarize yourself with the island's emergency procedures and evacuation routes in case of unforeseen events.

8. COVID-19 Considerations:
In 2023, as the world continues to navigate the effects of the pandemic, staying updated on COVID-19 guidelines and restrictions is crucial. Before you travel, check the latest travel advisories, testing requirements, and vaccination policies for entering Mykonos. Additionally, respect any local health protocols, such as wearing masks indoors or in crowded areas.

By prioritizing your safety and well-being during your Mykonos adventure, you'll have the freedom to fully enjoy the island's beauty, culture, and vibrant energy. Remember that a well-prepared traveler is a confident traveler, and with the right precautions, you'll create lasting memories while exploring this enchanting Aegean paradise in 2023.

Staying Connected: Internet and Communication

The desire to stay connected when traveling is more crucial than ever in the connected world of today. Mykonos, which is renowned for its tranquil beauty and energetic vibe, is aware of this. We'll go into the specifics of how you may easily remain connected, use the internet, and successfully communicate while on your Mykonos journey in this part.

1. Internet Access in Mykonos:
Mykonos has embraced the digital age, ensuring that visitors can remain online and connected. Whether you're updating your social media with stunning Aegean vistas or researching local hotspots, staying connected is convenient and hassle-free.

- Hotels and Accommodations: The majority of hotels, resorts, and vacation rentals on the island provide complimentary Wi-Fi to their guests. From luxurious resorts overlooking the sea to cozy boutique lodgings, you'll find a reliable internet connection that allows you to work, play, or plan your daily adventures.

- Public Spaces: Mykonos Town, with its enchanting labyrinth of streets and squares, boasts several public Wi-Fi hotspots. Cafes, promenades, and squares are often equipped with free Wi-Fi, allowing you to share your explorations in real-time or check your emails while savoring a Greek coffee.

- Mobile Data: To maintain connectivity beyond your accommodation and popular tourist areas, consider getting a local SIM card from one of the island's mobile providers. This option not only provides you with internet access but also lets you make local calls and send texts. Whether you're at a hidden beach or an off-the-beaten-path village, you'll have a reliable connection.

2. Effective Communication Tools:
In Mykonos, effective communication tools are essential for interacting with fellow travelers, locals, and service providers. These tools ensure that you can navigate the island's offerings seamlessly.

- Local SIM Cards: Acquiring a local SIM card offers the advantage of both data access and affordable local calls. This can prove invaluable when making reservations, coordinating plans, or reaching out to local businesses. You can easily purchase these SIM cards from various providers upon arrival at the airport or in Mykonos Town.

- Messaging Apps: Utilizing popular messaging apps like WhatsApp and Viber is a common practice in Mykonos. These apps enable you to make voice and video calls, send text messages, and even share your location with pinpoint accuracy. This is particularly useful for keeping in touch with fellow travelers or reaching out to local services.

- Language Translation Apps: While English is widely spoken in tourist-centric areas, having a language translation app can foster more meaningful interactions with locals. Apps like Google Translate allow you to bridge language barriers and engage in conversations that go beyond the surface.

3. Tips for Staying Connected:

- Consult Your Provider: Before your journey, it's advisable to contact your mobile provider to understand their international roaming plans and associated costs. While roaming options have improved over time, they may not always be the most economical solution.

- Prudent Use of Public Wi-Fi: While public Wi-Fi networks are convenient for staying connected, exercise caution when accessing sensitive information such as online banking or personal accounts. If you need to transmit sensitive data, consider using a virtual private network (VPN) to ensure the security of your connection.

- Download Offline Maps: Although Mykonos boasts reliable internet access, it's wise to download offline maps via apps like Google Maps. This preparation ensures that you can navigate even if you temporarily lose a data connection, allowing you to continue exploring the island with ease.

In the enchanting embrace of Mykonos, staying connected means you can capture and share every unforgettable moment, from the breathtaking sunrise over the Aegean to the festive nightlife in Mykonos Town. Embracing digital connectivity enhances your travel experience, allowing you to remain informed, engaged, and connected throughout your Mykonos journey.

Chapter 2

Embracing Enchanting Mykonos Town

Embracing Mykonos's enchanting town The hub of the island, Mykonos Town, or "Chora," is a mesmerizing maze of cobblestone lanes, bright white houses covered with colorful bougainvillaea, and an undeniable appeal that draws tourists from all over the world. Take in the charm of this little town, where modernity, culture, and history all coexist together.

Chora's Mesmerizing White-Washed Beauty

The lovely hamlet of Chora, located in the center of Mykonos, perfectly captures the ageless beauty and unique attractiveness of the island. Chora, commonly referred to as Mykonos Town, is a striking kaleidoscope of gleaming whitewashed structures, winding alleyways, and vivid bursts of color. This part goes deeply into Chora's beautiful beauty, revealing its undiscovered jewels, enduring landmarks, and the alluring ambiance that has attracted tourists for ages.

The White-Washed Canvas: A Timeless Aesthetic

Chora's signature look is a breathtaking display of white-washed buildings adorned with accents of blue, red, and earthy tones. This traditional Cycladic architecture isn't just for show; it serves a practical purpose. The white exterior reflects the sun's rays, keeping the buildings cool during the scorching Mediterranean summers. Wandering through these narrow streets feels like stepping into a dream, where every corner holds the promise of an unforgettable sight.

Discovering the Labyrinthine Alleys:

Chora's layout is intentionally intricate, designed to confuse pirates in ancient times and delight modern-day explorers. As you navigate the labyrinthine alleys, you'll encounter charming boutiques, art galleries, and inviting cafes at every turn. The alleys often lead to cozy squares and hidden corners where you can pause to soak in the ambiance. Don't hesitate to lose yourself in these passages; each twist and turn reveals a new facet of Chora's enchantment.

The Windmills of Mykonos: An Iconic Landmark:

Perched atop a hill overlooking Chora and the sea, the iconic Mykonos windmills stand as a testament to the island's history. Originally used to mill wheat, these windmills are now a beloved symbol of Mykonos. The sight of their white cylindrical forms silhouetted against the azure sky is an image that epitomizes the island's charm. Sunset is the best time to visit, as the windmills offer a panoramic view of the town bathed in the golden hues of twilight.

Captivating Views from Alefkandra Square:

As the sun dips below the horizon, Chora's Alefkandra Square comes alive. Known as "Little Venice," this waterfront area is a tapestry of quaint houses and restaurants that seem to float on the edge of the sea. It's a romantic haven where you can dine by the water's edge or sip a cocktail while the waves gently lap against the buildings. The vantage point offers stunning views of the Mykonos windmills and the picturesque seafront, creating an atmosphere that's nothing short of magical.

Preserving Chora's Timeless Charm:

While Chora has evolved to cater to modern travelers, it's heartening to see that the town has managed to preserve its authentic character. The strict building regulations that mandate the iconic white-washed look ensure that the town retains its unique identity. Exploring Chora isn't just about sightseeing; it's an opportunity to immerse yourself in a living piece of history, where tradition and contemporary influences blend seamlessly.

The Enchantment of Cycladic Architecture:
Chora's architecture is a living testament to the island's history and cultural heritage. The charming cubic houses with their flat roofs and blue-domed churches are quintessentially Cycladic. This architectural style isn't just about aesthetics; it's a reflection of the islanders' resourcefulness and adaptation to their environment. As you meander through the alleys, you'll notice the harmony between the buildings and the natural surroundings, creating a serene and visually pleasing atmosphere.

Artistry in the Details:
Every corner of Chora reveals intricate details that narrate the island's story. Wooden doors painted in shades of blue, bougainvillea cascading over walls, and cobblestone paths leading to hidden squares—all these elements contribute to Chora's beguiling charm. The narrow streets also serve as a canvas for local

artists, with colorful murals and street art adding an extra layer of creativity to the town's aesthetic.

Exploring the Shopping Delights:
Chora isn't just about its architectural marvels; it's also a shopper's paradise. Boutiques and galleries line the streets, offering everything from handmade jewelry and ceramics to fashion inspired by the island's breezy style. Whether you're looking for a unique keepsake or a piece of local art to adorn your home, Chora's shops provide an array of choices that are sure to captivate your senses.

A Gastronomic Journey Through Chora:
The town's culinary scene is as diverse as its architecture. Traditional tavernas serve up authentic Greek cuisine, from hearty moussaka to fresh seafood caught in the Aegean waters. Chora is also home to innovative eateries that fuse local ingredients with international flavors, creating a gastronomic experience that's a feast for both the eyes and the palate. Exploring the

town's dining options is like embarking on a journey that introduces you to the soul of Greek cuisine.

Cultural Landmarks and Hidden Gems:
Beyond the enchanting streets, Chora boasts cultural landmarks that invite you to delve deeper into the island's history. The Mykonos Archaeological Museum showcases artifacts that span centuries, providing insight into the island's ancient roots. The Folklore Museum offers a glimpse into traditional island life, from intricate textiles to historic photographs. Chora's vibrancy extends to its churches as well, with the Church of Panagia Paraportiani—a stunning example of Cycladic architecture—captivating visitors with its timeless beauty.

A Timeless Ambiance:

Chora's allure isn't confined to a particular time of day; it evolves as the sun arcs across the sky. In the early morning, the town is bathed in gentle sunlight, providing the perfect canvas for leisurely exploration. As the day progresses, the narrow streets become a shade-dappled sanctuary from the heat, inviting you to uncover every nook and cranny. Come evening, Chora transforms into a lively hub of activity as cafes, restaurants, and bars come alive with the island's spirited nightlife.

Chora's mesmerizing white-washed beauty isn't just a visual spectacle; it's an immersive experience that engages all your senses. From the architectural marvels that echo history to the vibrant shops, delectable cuisine, and cultural landmarks, Chora offers a rich tapestry of experiences. As you lose yourself in its charming alleys and embrace its timeless ambiance, you'll find that Chora isn't just a place on the map; it's a chapter in your journey through Mykonos.

Windmills and Panoramic Views

Experience Mykonos' ageless attraction as we explore the fascinating world of the island's recognizable windmills and the beautiful panoramas they provide. These windmills, perched on hills overlooking the aquamarine Aegean Sea, bear witness to the island's extensive history and distinctive architectural heritage.

The Windmills: Guardians of Mykonos' Past

The windmills of Mykonos have long been synonymous with the island's identity. Historically, they played a crucial role in the island's economy, serving as grinding mills for wheat and barley. Their distinctive cylindrical shapes, white walls, and conical roofs stand out against the azure skies, creating a postcard-worthy scene that has been celebrated in art, literature, and countless photographs.

Historical Significance and Architecture:
Dating back to the 16th century, the windmills were strategically built to harness the strong Cycladic winds that sweep across the island. Positioned to face the north, the windmills were designed to capture the prevailing winds, using their massive sails to turn grindstones within, producing flour for local consumption and trade.

Each windmill comprises three main levels. The ground floor served as a storage space for the grain, while the middle floor contained the machinery for grinding. The uppermost floor, crowned by the characteristic conical roof, housed the living quarters of the miller and his family. As you explore these structures, you'll discover the intricate wooden mechanisms that have weathered the passage of time, preserving the island's milling heritage.

Panoramic Views: A Glimpse of Mykonos' Beauty

Positioned at elevated points, the windmills offer some of the most alluring panoramic views on the island, in addition to their historical significance. As you climb the hills to reach the windmills, you'll be rewarded with sweeping vistas that encompass the glistening sea, the white-washed buildings of Mykonos Town, and the neighboring Cyclades islands.

The Magic of Sunset and Photography:

Among the many highlights of Mykonos' windmills is their role as prime sunset viewing spots. As the sun dips below the horizon, the sky transforms into a canvas of hues ranging from warm oranges to soft pinks. The windmills' silhouettes against this vibrant backdrop create an enchanting scene that beckons photographers and romantics alike.

Exploring the Windmills: Practical Tips

To fully embrace the charm of the windmills and their panoramic views, consider the following tips:

- Begin your journey in the late afternoon to witness the sunset from this vantage point.
- Wear comfortable shoes as some paths leading to the windmills might be uneven.
- Bring your camera or smartphone to capture the beauty of the surroundings.
- Respect the historical value of the windmills by not climbing on or touching them.

Preserving Mykonos' Windmills:

As you bask in the beauty and history of Mykonos' windmills, it's important to support efforts aimed at their preservation. These iconic structures are not only a testament to the island's past but also an integral part of its present identity. By visiting and respecting these landmarks, you contribute to the ongoing preservation of Mykonos' rich heritage.

Capturing the Essence: The Windmills' Enduring Allure

Mykonos' windmills continue to be a lasting representation of the island's ties to the land and the sea. The Cycladic architectural style that characterizes the island is exemplified by its bold white features against the dark blue background. The whispers of the millers' discussions, the creaking of wooden gears, and the rhythmic sounds of labor that once filled the air can almost be heard as you stand amidst these ancient buildings.

These days, instead of serving a useful role in fine grinding grain, windmills serve as iconic icons that bring tourists from all over the world. The spiritual aura they emit as well as its historical significance entices visitors. These windmills seem to be preserving the soul of Mykonos and telling its tales to those who are open to hearing them.

Exploring Beyond the Windmills: A Sense of Place

The road to get there is just as gratifying as the windmills themselves, which are a magnificent attraction. As you meander around Mykonos Town's maze-like alleyways, you'll find yourself surrounded by a setting that perfectly embodies the character of the island. The bougainvillea-draped whitewashed homes, the alleyways that appear to lead to hidden treasures, and the sounds of laughter from neighborhood cafés all add to the island of Mykonos' vivid tapestry.

The huge Aegean Sea and the nearby islands gradually come into view as you go closer to the windmills. This region's connection is demonstrated by the windmills' current function as cultural connectors, which connect the past to the present and invite visitors to take part in their heritage. Historically, windmills served as essential grinding machines.

Reflection and Contemplation: Sunset at the Windmills

The windmills transcend their status as architectural wonders when the sun starts to set over the horizon and casts warm colors across the sky. They turn into places for introspection and thought, encouraging you to take a moment to see the beauty all around you. A moment of connection with nature and history is provided by the peaceful spirit of these buildings paired with the peace of the surrounding scenery, serving as a reminder of the enduring cycles that mold the island and its visitors.

Preserving the Legacy: Your Role as a Traveler

It's important to think about your contribution to their preservation when you explore the windmills in Mykonos. It is our duty as travelers to handle these historical sites with respect and care since they contain tales that date back hundreds of years. Make sure future generations may enjoy the allure of Mykonos' windmills by admiring their beauty, photographing them, and leaving only footprints behind.

A Connection Across Time and Place

The windmills of Mykonos are more than just architectural features; they are doors into a world where the past and the present dwell together. With each step you take in the direction of these well-known sites, you go across time and space as well as through actual space. You are invited by the windmills to leave the bustle of everyday life and enter a world where simplicity, beauty, and a closeness to nature rule.

Remember the windmills as you leave this gorgeous area; they stand alert and provide a feeling of stability in a world that is always changing. They perfectly capture the spirit of Mykonos, a location where innovation and tradition coexist with legacy and adventure against the background of the glistening Aegean Sea. You participate in a story that transcends centuries in this timeless encounter. This story, like the windmills themselves, keeps spinning and will continue to do so for a long time to come.

Exploring Little Venice's Bohemian Charm

The alluring neighborhood known as "Little Venice" is located in Mykonos Town and is tucked away at the edge of the ocean. Here, visitors may explore a world of magic, creative expression, and a compelling history tale. The heart of Little Venice is explored in this part, where the seductive fusion of breathtaking panoramas, creative energy, and seashore attraction creates a unique experience.

1. The Allure of Little Venice: A Seaside Fantasy Come to Life
The enchantment of Little Venice lies in its exquisite architecture, where quaint houses in a spectrum of colors perch on the water's edge. Evoking images of the Italian city it's named after, this waterfront district exudes a romantic

ambiance that ignites the imagination. The houses, characterized by their wooden balconies that seem to embrace the Aegean Sea, create a picturesque setting that has been immortalized by countless artists and photographers. The symphony of sea breeze and waves against the buildings provides an immersive soundscape that further enhances the ethereal atmosphere. Meandering through the maze of narrow alleys, you'll find every corner holds a new perspective of this stunning marriage of architecture and natural beauty.

2. Captivating Sunset Views: Nature's Canvas in Little Venice

One of the undeniable highlights of Little Venice is its unparalleled vantage point for witnessing the spectacular Mykonos sunsets. As the sun dips toward the horizon, a mesmerizing panorama of warm hues and gentle reflections takes center stage. The scene is beautifully complemented by the swaying palm trees, the iconic windmills silhouetted against the sky, and the tranquil sea, creating a symphony of sights and sounds that stir the soul. Whether you choose to experience this spectacle from a cozy rooftop terrace, a seaside cafe, or the inviting stone steps that descend into the Aegean waters, the transition from day to night in Little Venice is nothing short of enchanting.

3. Quaint Cafes and Seaside Dining: A Gastronomic Journey by the Water

The culinary tapestry of Little Venice is a blend of delectable flavors and stunning views, with the district's cafes and restaurants offering an exceptional dining experience that perfectly complements the maritime ambiance. Savor the catch of the day as you indulge in freshly prepared seafood, Mediterranean delicacies, and international cuisines that cater to every palate. What makes dining here truly exceptional, however, is the proximity to the sea. As you savor each bite, the gentle sea breeze and the rhythmic sound of waves create a sensory symphony that enhances the flavors and transforms a meal into an unforgettable experience.

4. Artistic Vibes and Creative Expression: Where Inspiration Flourishes

Beyond its aesthetic allure, Little Venice is a haven for artists, musicians, and creative minds who find inspiration in its bohemian atmosphere. Art galleries dot the district, showcasing a blend of local and international works that reflect the vibrant cultural scene of Mykonos. These galleries serve as gateways to artistic exploration, inviting visitors to immerse themselves in the visual narratives that artists from around the world bring to life. In addition to visual arts, the district is a hub for live music performances that resonate with the rhythm of the sea. Whether you're an artist seeking inspiration or an enthusiast of creative expression, Little Venice offers an atmosphere that nurtures imagination and celebrates artistic diversity.

5. Shopping and Boutiques: Discovering Unique Treasures

Little Venice's eclectic charm extends to its collection of boutique shops, each offering a curated selection of fashion, accessories, and one-of-a-kind souvenirs. From handcrafted jewelry that captures the essence of Mykonos to stylish beachwear that embodies the island's carefree spirit, these boutiques provide an opportunity to acquire distinctive pieces that serve as tangible reminders of your journey. As you browse through these stores, you'll find that each item carries a touch of Mykonos' artistic character, making shopping an experience that connects you to the island's essence.

6. Nightlife and Social Scene: From Sunset to Starlight Revelry

As night descends on Little Venice, the district transforms into a vibrant hub of nightlife and social interaction. The atmospheric transition from the golden hues of sunset to the twinkle of starlight is accompanied by the lively pulse of bars and clubs coming to life. The rhythm of music mingles with laughter and conversation, creating an atmosphere of celebration. Whether you seek a cozy spot to unwind with a cocktail or a lively venue to dance the night away, Little Venice's nocturnal scene offers a range of options that cater to different preferences.

7. Cultural and Historical Significance: A Tapestry of Heritage

Beyond its contemporary charm, Little Venice is imbued with historical significance that traces back to the island's maritime heritage. It is believed that the district was once home to sea captains and traders who constructed their residences along the water's edge. This strategic location facilitated the swift loading and unloading of goods, contributing to Mykonos' thriving maritime activity. The echoes of this history can still be felt in the architecture, where the houses' design reflects their functional role in the island's trade. As you explore Little Venice, you're not only immersing yourself in its modern allure but also unraveling a tapestry of heritage that tells the story of Mykonos' evolution over time.

A Journey into the Bohemian Soul of Mykonos: Little Venice is more than a collection of picturesque buildings; it's an experience that encapsulates the essence of Mykonos' bohemian spirit. The district's marriage of artistic expression, gastronomic delights, historical resonance, and natural beauty creates an immersive journey that lingers in your memory long after you've left its shores. Every sunset shared, every note of music heard, and every creative expression encountered becomes a fragment of the intricate mosaic that is Little Venice—a treasure trove of experiences that continue to inspire and enchant. As you depart from this captivating enclave, you carry with you the echoes of its enchantment, forever woven into the narrative of your Mykonos odyssey.

Icons Unveiled: Landmarks and Art Galleries

Chora, the name given to Mykonos Town, is a charming maze of cobblestone alleyways and whitewashed structures filled with vivid bougainvillaea. In addition to its attractive aesthetics, Chora is a treasure mine of famous sites and art galleries that depict the rich history and artistic expression of Mykonos.

1. The Windmills of Mykonos:
Standing tall and proud against the azure sky, the iconic Mykonos windmills are among the island's most recognizable symbols. These windmills were once integral to the island's economy, serving as grain mills to harness the power of the winds that swept through Mykonos. Today, they stand as silent sentinels, offering breathtaking panoramic views of the town and the Aegean Sea. Sunset is an especially magical

time to visit, as the windmills become silhouettes against the fiery hues of the sky.

2. The Archaeological Museum of Mykonos:
Delve into Mykonos' deep-rooted history by visiting the Archaeological Museum. Located in the heart of Chora, this museum houses a collection of artifacts spanning various historical periods, from the prehistoric to the Hellenistic era. Explore ancient pottery, sculptures, jewelry, and tools that provide insights into Mykonos' role in the ancient world. Of particular interest is the collection of artifacts from the nearby island of Delos, a UNESCO World Heritage site that was once a bustling center of trade and culture.

3. Lena's House Folk Museum:
Step back in time and experience the traditional Mykonian way of life at Lena's House Folk Museum. Housed in a preserved 19th-century captain's mansion, the museum offers a glimpse into the island's past. Explore furnished rooms showcasing period furniture, traditional costumes, and household items. Each corner of

the museum exudes authenticity, giving visitors an intimate understanding of Mykonos' cultural heritage.

4. Rarity Gallery:

For art enthusiasts, Rarity Gallery stands as a testament to Mykonos' contemporary creative scene. This art space showcases a curated selection of contemporary paintings, sculptures, and other artworks by both Greek and international artists. The gallery's collection reflects the fusion of Mykonos' traditional charm and modern artistic expression, offering visitors a chance to engage with the island's evolving cultural landscape.

5. Agricultural Museum Boni Windmill:

Discover the island's agrarian roots at the Agricultural Museum Boni Windmill. This unique museum is housed within a restored windmill and offers visitors an insight into Mykonos' agricultural practices. From traditional farming tools to displays on the cultivation of crops in the island's challenging terrain, the museum highlights the resilience of Mykonos' farming community.

6. The Mykonos Municipal Art Gallery:
Nurturing the island's artistic spirit, the Mykonos Municipal Art Gallery is a hub for creativity and cultural exploration. The gallery features a diverse collection of artworks, ranging from classical to contemporary, showcasing the talents of local artists. Rotating exhibitions ensure that every visit brings new perspectives and artistic inspirations.

7. The Panagia Paraportiani Church:
One of the most unique and photographed churches in Mykonos, the Panagia Paraportiani is a stunning architectural marvel. Comprising a complex of five chapels, the church's distinctive design is a fusion of different architectural styles, showcasing the island's rich history and influences. The stark white exterior against the backdrop of the blue sky and sea creates an ethereal beauty that is truly mesmerizing.

8. Aegean Maritime Museum:

With its strong maritime heritage, Mykonos pays homage to its seafaring legacy at the Aegean Maritime Museum. This museum is home to an impressive collection of ship models, navigational instruments, historical documents, and artifacts that chronicle the island's maritime history. Of special note is the historic "Armenistis" lighthouse lantern, which once guided sailors safely through the treacherous waters.

9. Matoyianni Street:

More than just a street, Matoyianni is an experience. This bustling narrow street in Chora is a shopaholic's paradise, lined with boutique stores, art galleries, cafes, and artisan shops. Stroll along Matoyianni Street to discover local craftsmanship, fashion, jewelry, and souvenirs that reflect the island's unique aesthetic. The vibrant energy and colorful storefronts make it a must-visit for anyone looking to indulge in retail therapy.

10. The Folklore Museum of Mykonos:
Immerse yourself in the island's traditional culture and heritage at the Folklore Museum of Mykonos. Housed in an 18th-century captain's house, this museum offers a comprehensive look at Mykonos' customs, daily life, and cultural traditions. Explore a collection of artifacts that include traditional clothing, tools, musical instruments, and household items, all of which provide insights into the island's deep-rooted identity.

11. Rarity Gallery Sculpture Garden:
Extending the artistic experience beyond the gallery walls, the Rarity Gallery Sculpture Garden invites visitors to engage with contemporary sculptures in an outdoor setting. This tranquil oasis showcases a collection of sculptures crafted by both emerging and established artists. The serene environment enhances the appreciation of the artworks, offering a unique blend of nature and creativity.

12. Tria Pigadia: The Three Wells:

Tria Pigadia, meaning "Three Wells," is a charming square in Chora that encapsulates the essence of Mykonos' history. In the past, the square was a vital water source for the town. Today, it's a picturesque spot adorned with colorful flowers, surrounded by cafes and restaurants. Its quaint beauty invites visitors to relax, people-watch, and savor the timeless atmosphere.

13. Mykonos Agricultural Museum:

Venture into the heart of Mykonos' rural heritage at the Agricultural Museum. Housed within a traditional stone building, this museum showcases the island's agricultural traditions. From ancient tools to exhibits on farming techniques, visitors can discover the dedication and resourcefulness that sustained Mykonos' agrarian communities for generations.

14. The Municipal Library of Mykonos:

For those seeking intellectual enrichment, the Municipal Library of Mykonos offers a serene escape. This haven of knowledge boasts an impressive collection of books, manuscripts, and historical documents. Whether you're a literature lover or a researcher, the library's offerings provide a window into Mykonos' intellectual pursuits and literary heritage.

15. Panagia Tourliani Monastery:

A short journey outside Chora takes you to the Panagia Tourliani Monastery, a spiritual and architectural masterpiece. Adorned with intricate woodcarvings and Byzantine icons, the monastery's interior is a testament to Mykonos' devotion and cultural craftsmanship. The monastery's courtyard, with its vibrant garden and iconic bell tower, offers a tranquil retreat for contemplation.

16. Mykonos Marina:

While often overlooked as a landmark, the Mykonos Marina plays a pivotal role in the island's maritime identity. Wander along its promenade and watch as yachts and fishing boats sway in harmony with the sea. The marina's vibrant energy showcases the island's connection to the Aegean waters and its enduring allure to seafaring enthusiasts.

17. Mykonos Town Galleries:
Beyond individual galleries, the entirety of Mykonos Town is an open-air gallery, where the streets themselves become a canvas for artistic expression. Colorful murals, intricate graffiti, and creative street art punctuate the town's narrow alleys. Embark on an urban art exploration, uncovering hidden gems at every turn and celebrating the island's contemporary artistic spirit.

18. Rarity Gallery Sculpture Park:
Elevating the art scene, the Rarity Gallery Sculpture Park invites visitors to engage with sculptures against the backdrop of Mykonos' natural beauty. The park is a sanctuary of creativity, where sculptures come to life amidst lush gardens. As you wander the paths, each sculpture offers a unique perspective, blending

artistic interpretation with the island's scenic splendor.

19. Armenistis Lighthouse:

Perched on the northern tip of Mykonos, the Armenistis Lighthouse stands as a beacon of history and maritime heritage. The lighthouse has witnessed centuries of seafaring stories and offers panoramic views of the surrounding landscape and the endless sea. As the sun sets over the Aegean, the lighthouse provides a breathtaking vantage point for nature's grand spectacle.

The landmarks and art galleries of Mykonos Town tell a tale of a multifaceted island—a tapestry woven with history, creativity, and cultural significance. Each site, whether an ancient windmill or a contemporary art space, contributes to Mykonos' narrative, inviting visitors to immerse themselves in the island's diverse and captivating identity. As you explore these sites, you'll not only admire the craftsmanship but also connect with the essence of Mykonos itself, leaving you with cherished memories of a truly enchanting destination.

Sunset Delights at Alefkandra Square

The transition from day to night in Mykonos Town's Alefkandra Square is a magical metamorphosis that paints the sky with hues of gold and orange, and this section invites you to immerse yourself in the captivating beauty and vibrant energy of one of Mykonos' most enchanting spots for watching the sunset.

1. Alefkandra Square: A Gathering of Beauty and Culture

Alefkandra Square affectionately referred to as "Little Venice," is a masterpiece that marries Cycladic architecture with coastal allure. Named after the resemblance it bears to the iconic Italian city of Venice, this picturesque square is a cluster of colorful buildings, each adorned with charming balconies that seem to extend their embrace over the azure waters of the Aegean Sea. The narrow alleys winding through the square add a touch of mystery and intrigue, inviting exploration and discovery.

2. Sunset Serenity and Atmosphere

As the day gracefully turns into evening, the atmosphere in Alefkandra Square undergoes a profound transformation. The gentle whispers of the Aegean waves create a soothing symphony that accompanies the breathtaking sunset. Whether you choose to recline in a cozy cafe corner, stroll along the water's edge, or stand pensively on one of the quaint bridges that connect the buildings, you're enveloped in an atmosphere of serenity and awe, where time seems to slow down.

3. Capturing the Perfect Moment

Alefkandra Square is a haven for avid photographers and casual snappers alike. The setting sun's warm embrace casts a soft, golden glow upon the tranquil waters, orchestrating a mesmerizing dance of colors that envelop the surroundings. As the sun's angle shifts, the buildings' unique architecture comes alive in a tapestry of shadows and reflections, offering a visual feast that beckons to be captured. Whether you wield a professional camera or a smartphone, Alefkandra Square provides an endless canvas of inspiration.

4. Enjoying the Culinary Scene

An experience at Alefkandra Square would be incomplete without indulging in its culinary offerings that perfectly complement the enchanting sunset. The square boasts an array of cafes, bars, and restaurants, each carving a niche with its distinct ambiance and flavors. Savor a signature cocktail as the sun dips below the horizon or relish in delectable seafood dishes, showcasing the freshest catches of the day. With the sun's descent, the culinary journey mirrors the transition from day to night, creating an exquisite fusion of tastes and senses.

5. Cultural Connections and Entertainment

Beyond its physical charm, Alefkandra Square fosters cultural connections and spontaneous entertainment. Street musicians and performers often gather to contribute to the magnetic ambiance. Locals and visitors alike converge, sharing stories, laughter, and moments, nurturing the sense of community that the square effortlessly conjures. Engaging with the locals and fellow travelers offers an opportunity to create meaningful connections and to partake in the vibrant spirit of Mykonos.

6. Sunset Rituals and Mykonos' Magic

Observing the sunset at Alefkandra Square becomes a ritual that many cherish during their time on the island. The slow retreat of the sun symbolizes a transition not only from day to night but also from the past to the present. It's a moment that encapsulates the beauty of embracing the fleeting nature of time and savoring each passing instant. As the sun dips below the horizon, the square's lights come alive, illuminating the night ahead and infusing it with an aura of enchantment.

7. Insider Tips for the Perfect Experience

- Arrive Early: To secure a prime spot and to fully immerse yourself in the evolving atmosphere, arrive at Alefkandra Square well before the sun begins its descent.
- Dine by the Sea: Enhance your experience by booking a table at one of the waterfront restaurants, where you can savor a romantic candlelit dinner against the backdrop of the sunset.
- Capture the Beauty: Experiment with various angles and compositions to capture the essence of the sunset's changing colors and the square's unique architecture.
- Explore After Dark: After the sun has set and the stars begin to twinkle, take a stroll through the charming alleys adjacent to the square,

uncovering hidden treasures and enjoying the serene ambiance.

Alefkandra Square's sunset show is a symphony of sights, sounds, and feelings as the sun sinks below the horizon. Mykonos' architecture, the calm sea, and the feeling of community all work together to tell the island's story. A new period of the day begins with the sun's final bow and the square's illumination, one that will continue to attract people long after the sun has set. Keep the magic of this event close to your heart as a treasured reminder of Mykonos' enduring attraction.

Chapter 3

Beaches of Mykonos: Sun, Sea, and Serenity

Psarou Beach: Luxury and Glamour

Psarou Beach, which is tucked away like a gem on Mykonos' shoreline, reveals itself to be a lavish and glamorous paradise. We'll go deep into the magic of Psarou Beach in this thorough tour, where the attraction of luxury coexists peacefully with the Aegean Sea's unmatched beauty.

1. A Glimpse of Paradise on Earth
Psarou Beach transcends the conventional definition of a seaside destination—it is, in fact, a pocket of paradise on Earth. As your feet press

into the soft, powdery sands, an immediate sense of exclusivity and indulgence embraces you. The glistening turquoise waters stretching before you and the awe-inspiring vistas in the distance paint a picture of ethereal beauty. Psarou Beach isn't just a place; it's an experience that embodies the quintessence of Mykonos.

2. Luxurious Lounging and VIP Treatment

What distinguishes Psarou Beach from ordinary shores is its commitment to luxury that borders on artistry. The beach clubs and lounges that adorn its fringes redefine relaxation. Here, exclusive cabanas, cushioned sunbeds, and a team of attentive staff cater to your every whim, creating an atmosphere of unadulterated comfort. Whether you're sipping a bespoke cocktail, reclining under the shade of a billowing umbrella, or feeling the gentle caress of the sea breeze on your skin, Psarou Beach elevates relaxation to an unparalleled art form.

3. Celeb-Spotting and A-List Atmosphere

Psarou Beach enjoys a reputation that reaches beyond the borders of Mykonos—a reputation that has made it a magnet for celebrities and global trendsetters. It's not an uncommon occurrence to share the sands with Hollywood stars, chart-topping musicians, and influential personalities who are drawn to the allure of Psarou. The air carries a distinct A-list atmosphere, where every moment feels like a scene from an opulent movie, and every encounter seems to be taken from a page of a glamorous novel.

4. Gastronomic Delights by the Sea

Yet, Psarou Beach is not limited to the splendor of its sands and waves. It is a culinary haven that tantalizes the taste buds as much as it mesmerizes the eyes. The beachfront restaurants and tavernas offer a sensory journey through an array of dishes. From the earthy flavors of traditional Greek cuisine to the cosmopolitan tastes of international fare, Psarou's culinary scene is a symphony of flavors and textures. Imagine indulging in a plate of freshly caught seafood while your gaze sweeps across the Aegean's expansive azure canvas—a dining experience that engages all the senses.

5. Water Adventures and Aquatic Pleasures

However, Psarou Beach doesn't just allure with its luxurious comforts and exquisite dining—it also invites you to explore the vibrant world beneath its crystalline waves. The cerulean waters that lap the shore are a gateway to underwater wonders. Snorkeling unveils an underwater realm teeming with life, and swimming offers a sensory embrace of the Aegean's gentle currents. For the more adventurous, a plethora of water sports await—jet skiing, paddle boarding, and diving into the depths where treasures of the deep await your discovery.

6. Iconic Parties and Mykonos' Nightlife

As the sun's descent paints the sky with hues of pink and gold, Psarou Beach dons a new identity—a pulsating heart of nightlife and celebration. The beach clubs and bars come to life with music that merges with the rhythm of the waves, laughter that dances on the breeze, and the clinking of glasses that raise a toast to the night. Sunset parties and beachfront soirées become the canvas for unforgettable memories, and the energy that courses through the air captures the vivacious spirit that defines Mykonos' nightlife.

7. Tips for the Ultimate Psarou Experience

- Early Arrival: To secure your spot on the sought-after shores of Psarou Beach, it's advisable to arrive early, especially during the peak seasons.
- Reservations for Elegance: For an experience that resonates with luxury, consider making reservations for exclusive cabanas or sunbeds.

- Exploring the Underwater World: Don't miss the opportunity to snorkel and immerse yourself in the underwater wonderland that lies just beneath the surface.
- Sample Local Culinary Delights: Delight in the authenticity of Greek flavors by indulging in traditional dishes served at the beachfront tavernas.

Psarou Beach stands as a testament to Mykonos' unique ability to harmonize the lavish with the natural. Here, luxury isn't just a concept—it's a lifestyle where the embrace of the Aegean and the lap of the waves against the shore are the rhythms of opulence. As you recline in comfort, dance the night away, or plunge into the sea's embrace, Psarou Beach invites you to experience the allure of Mykonos in its most refined and captivating form.

Paradise Beach: Vibrant Parties and Clear Waters

Enter the vibrant world of Paradise Beach, a true hub of lively activity and crystal-clear azure seas. This section reveals the vibrant center of Mykonos' party scene, where the pulse of the music fuses with the soothing lapping of the sea to create an enduringly joyful ambiance.

1. The Playground of Partygoers

Paradise Beach, which is located on Mykonos' southern shore, is a popular vacation spot. The beach transforms into a magical playground for people looking for a never-ending party the minute the sun peaks over the horizon. The beach has a well-deserved reputation as a hopping party destination since it welcomes partygoers of all stripes, ensuring that the city's pulse never stops.

2. The Beach Club Experience

Paradise Beach's allure goes beyond the sun, sea, and sand; it is a sanctuary of sensory indulgence. At its heart lies the concept of beach clubs that redefine beachside entertainment. Lavish lounges adorned with vibrant colors, plush sunbeds, and attentive service create an atmosphere that seamlessly transitions from tranquil relaxation during the day to electrifying revelry as the sun sets. With iconic beach clubs gracing the shoreline, such as the legendary Tropicana Club, each visitor is invited to be part of a living, breathing symphony of music, movement, and merriment.

3. Dancing in the Sand and Beyond

Dancing is an integral part of the Paradise Beach experience. The golden sands transform into dance floors, allowing visitors to let their inhibitions loose under the open sky. The energy is contagious; it's a place where strangers become friends through shared dance and shared joy. The Tropicana Club, renowned for its dancing-on-the-bar parties, invites you to let your inner dancer shine. As the sun paints the horizon with hues of gold, the music takes over, and the beach pulsates to the rhythm of celebration.

4. Crystal-clear waters and Beachside Comfort

Amidst the spirited celebrations, Paradise Beach retains its natural elegance. The sea's clear blue expanse, almost mirroring the sky above, offers a refreshing escape from the dance floor. The waters invite you to plunge into their soothing embrace, providing a rejuvenating break from the high-energy festivities. The soft sands remain an inviting option for those who wish to lounge by the water's edge, enjoying the gentle sea breeze and the sound of the waves.

5. A Global Gathering

Paradise Beach transcends boundaries, serving as a global gathering point where cultures collide and stories intertwine. Here, individuals from diverse backgrounds share the common language of celebration. It's a place where connections are formed, conversations flow freely, and friendships emerge from shared laughter and shared experiences. Mykonos' reputation as an international hub of camaraderie and festivity comes to life on this vibrant stretch of shoreline.

6. Gastronomic Delights and Refreshing Libations

The beach's energy isn't confined to the dance floor—it extends to the culinary scene as well. A collection of beachfront restaurants and bars provides a plethora of culinary delights, catering to diverse palates. Indulge in traditional Greek dishes crafted from the freshest ingredients, or explore international cuisines that cater to every taste. Quench your thirst with signature cocktails and refreshing beverages, perfectly complementing the beachside atmosphere.

7. Tips for Making the Most of Paradise Beach

- Early Arrival: To secure the best spot and make the most of the entire day's offerings, consider arriving early in the morning.
- Essential Gear: Pack essentials like sunscreen, comfortable footwear for dancing, and beachwear that allows you to transition from dancing to relaxation seamlessly.
- Embrace the Vibrant Vibe: Let go of inhibitions and fully immerse yourself in the energetic atmosphere. Dancing and mingling with fellow partygoers are integral parts of the experience.
- Stay Hydrated: Amid the excitement, remember to stay hydrated. Take breaks to rest and recharge, ensuring that you're able to enjoy the festivities to the fullest.

Paradise Beach is a miniature representation of Mykonos; it's where celebration and the island's breathtaking scenery come together to provide visitors with an unforgettable experience. Every element of Paradise Beach welcomes you to take part in an extraordinary celebration, from the entrancing music beat to the refreshing touch of the Aegean waves. You'll be enchanted by the stunning tapestry of happiness, laughing, and lively life that characterizes Mykonos' dynamic charm as the sun sets and the stars glitter overhead.

Super Paradise Beach: Entertainment and Celeb Sightings

Super Paradise Beach emerges as a dynamic sanctuary of liveliness, delivering an exuberant combination of energy, thrilling festivities, and the tantalizing chance of celebrity sightings, nestled within the embrace of Mykonos' crystal-clear waves. In this segment, we enter into the effervescent realm of Super Paradise, where the beach's essence pulses with a seductive charm, and the waves dance to their rhythm.

1. The Playful Playground of Super Paradise Beach

Super Paradise Beach isn't merely a stretch of sand and sea; it is a dynamic playground where the fusion of nature's gifts and human enthusiasm creates an atmosphere of boundless joy. The moment you set foot on its sun-kissed sands, you are greeted by an invigorating ambiance that resonates with the laughter of beachgoers and the gentle rhythm of waves brushing against the shore. The beach boasts a vibrant tapestry of colors and activities, transforming it into an open-air arena of pleasure and excitement.

2. Daytime Vibrancy: Fun in the Sun

As the sun ascends its zenith, Super Paradise awakens with a symphony of activities, each designed to cater to a spectrum of preferences. Water sports enthusiasts take to the Aegean's gentle waves, indulging in jet skiing, paddleboarding, and parasailing. The beach volleyball courts buzz with enthusiastic players, creating an atmosphere of friendly rivalry and shared camaraderie. For those seeking relaxation, the sunbeds offer a tranquil oasis for soaking up the rays, while beachside bars serve up refreshing concoctions to keep the spirits high.

3. Sunset Spectacles and Evening Magic

As the sun begins its descent beyond the horizon, Super Paradise undergoes a breathtaking transformation. The air becomes charged with anticipation as the sky becomes a canvas painted with shades of pink, orange, and gold. Sunset at Super Paradise is more than a transition from day to night; it's a spectacle that ignites the beach with renewed energy. The fading light casts a serene backdrop, heralding the arrival of the night's festivities.

4. A Celestial Entertainment Experience

Super Paradise Beach's reputation as a legendary party destination is well-deserved. As twilight fades into the inky night, the beach metamorphoses into an exhilarating dance floor illuminated by neon lights and laser beams. The crescendo of music fills the air, beckoning revelers to immerse themselves in a night of unparalleled euphoria. Renowned DJs and live music performances infuse the beach with electric energy, guiding the dance and celebration well into the wee hours.

5. Celebrities, Allure, and Connections

Super Paradise Beach transcends its status as a party hotspot—it's a magnet for celebrities, influencers, and those seeking an unforgettable experience. Amidst the pulsating music and vivacious atmosphere, it's not uncommon to spot familiar faces from the world of entertainment and fashion. Super Paradise's universal appeal draws visitors from diverse backgrounds, cultures, and countries, fostering a unique environment where connections and shared memories are forged.

6. Culinary Delights by the Shore

Amidst the whirlwind of excitement, Super Paradise ensures that culinary experiences remain a paramount delight. Beachfront establishments offer a diverse culinary landscape, ranging from traditional Greek fare to international culinary journeys. Picture yourself savoring freshly caught seafood while the Aegean breeze carries the aroma of the sea, or relishing in Mediterranean classics as the sun dips below the horizon—a culinary exploration that perfectly complements the vibrant spirit of the beach.

7. Tips for a Super Paradise Adventure

- Daytime Discovery: Immerse yourself in water sports, beach games, and relaxation during the day to embrace the beach's dynamic atmosphere.
- Sunset Reverie: Find a prime spot to witness the breathtaking sunset; let the changing colors of the sky mesmerize you.
- Nighttime Festivity: Dress comfortably and prepare for a night of dancing and celebration, embracing the exhilarating nightlife.
- VIP Indulgence: Consider exploring VIP packages provided by beach clubs for an enhanced experience.

Super Paradise Beach isn't merely a destination; it's an emotion, an experience that encapsulates the essence of Mykonos' vivacity. It's a place where the daylight's joy fuses seamlessly with the nighttime's exuberance, creating an indelible memory. With its dynamic energy, magnetic allure, and legendary parties, Super Paradise invites you to dance under the stars, revel in the music, and be part of a celebration that transcends time—a memory that lingers as a reminder of the heartbeat of Mykonos.

Elia Beach: Tranquil Escape and Crystal Sands

Elia Beach, which is tucked away on the beautiful island of Mykonos' southern shore, is a tranquil retreat where the calming murmur of the Aegean waves and the soft rustle of palm fronds blend. This section reveals Elia Beach's attractions and welcomes you to discover its special combination of peace, glittering beaches, and an atmosphere that promotes rest and renewal.

1. The Essence of Tranquility

Elia Beach boasts a rare gift—the ability to transport you from the bustling world to a realm of utter tranquility. Stepping onto its shores is akin to stepping into a sanctuary of serenity. As you set foot on its fine sands, a sense of calm envelops you, the worries of the everyday world slipping away with each footstep. The spaciousness of Elia Beach ensures that you can find your haven, whether you seek quiet contemplation, intimate conversations, or simply the space to lay your towel and soak in the sun.

2. Crystal Sands and Azure Waters

One of Elia Beach's defining features is its sands—a canvas of golden softness that stretches towards the horizon. The sands here are more than just a place to lie down; they are an invitation to immerse yourself in their warmth and embrace. The Aegean Sea, with its brilliant shades of blue, is a playground for the senses. The waters gently lap the shore, an invitation to wade in or dive for a refreshing swim. As you float in the sea's embrace, a feeling of weightlessness and freedom washes over you.

3. Secluded Bliss and Natural Beauty

Elia Beach offers an escape not just in the sense of tranquility, but also in its unique ability to provide a sense of privacy even during peak seasons. The spacious layout of the beach ensures that you can relish the pleasures of sunbathing, building sandcastles, or simply watching the horizon without the feeling of being crowded. The beach is framed by rugged hills, a natural backdrop that enhances the feeling of being cocooned in a hidden paradise, far removed from the cares of the world.

4. Beachside Dining and Culinary Pleasures

While the natural beauty of Elia Beach is awe-inspiring, it's also a gastronomic destination in its own right. Along the shoreline, a collection of beachside tavernas and restaurants beckon, offering an array of culinary treasures. Here, the symphony of waves meets the melody of sizzling pans and clinking cutlery. Fresh seafood, a jewel in Greek cuisine, takes center stage on many menus. From octopus grilled to perfection to platters of mezze, each dish becomes a culinary journey that's as visually appealing as it is delectable.

5. Water Adventures and Recreational Joy

For those whose sense of adventure seeks expression, Elia Beach presents an array of water-based activities to captivate and entertain. The calm waters that cradle the beach offer a canvas for exploration. Paddleboarding becomes a dance with the waves, while jet skiing adds a dash of exhilaration. Snorkeling is an invitation to peek beneath the surface and discover the vibrant marine world that calls the Aegean home. Regardless of your choice, Elia Beach transforms into a playground of aquatic wonder.

6. Unwind and Rejuvenate

Elia Beach, with its unhurried pace and serene vistas, extends an invitation to find solace and balance. The beach's ambiance lends itself to wellness and relaxation. Unroll a yoga mat and let the gentle sound of waves guide your practice, fostering a connection between body and environment. As the sun warms your skin, meditation becomes a journey inward, aided by the soothing rhythm of the sea. Whether you choose to indulge in yoga, meditation, or simply quiet contemplation, Elia Beach becomes a sanctuary for rejuvenation.

7. Tips for Maximizing Your Elia Experience

- Time Your Arrival: To secure a prime spot and make the most of your day, consider arriving early, particularly during peak seasons.
- Dine by the Shore: Explore the culinary offerings at the beachfront tavernas for a taste of local and Mediterranean flavors.
- Explore the Waters: Engage in water sports or take a leisurely swim to fully immerse yourself in the Aegean's embrace.
- Wellness Rituals: Pack a yoga mat and embrace the serenity of the beach to engage in wellness practices.

Elia Beach isn't just a stretch of sand; it's a portal to another dimension—a realm where the worries of the world fade and the essence of life is distilled into the gentle lapping of waves and the warm touch of the sun. As you stand on its sands, you're invited to embark on a journey of relaxation, exploration, and rejuvenation. The sands, the sea, the culinary delights, and the promise of adventure all blend to create an experience that captures the very essence of Mykonos' beach paradise.

Agios Sostis: Secluded Bliss and Natural Beauty

Agios Sostis is a hidden gem that has been waiting to be found. It is tucked away on the northern shore of Mykonos, away from the busy throng and commercial hum. This part offers a tranquil retreat from the island's busier beaches by delving further into the peace and untainted beauty that characterize Agios Sostis.

1. Unveiling the Secret Sanctuary

Agios Sostis is not just a beach; it's a sanctuary that beckons travelers seeking a more authentic and unadulterated experience. Often referred to as "Mykonos' Best-Kept Secret," this beach stands as a testament to the island's ability to preserve natural beauty while providing an escape from the ordinary. Here, you'll find a haven where untouched landscapes and tranquil shores come together in perfect harmony.

2. A Journey Off the Beaten Path

Visiting Agios Sostis is not just about arriving at a destination; it's about embarking on a journey that's as much internal as it is external. The path to the beach takes you through a scenic route that winds through rugged terrain, creating a sense of anticipation and adventure. The journey itself becomes an essential part of the experience, preparing you for the tranquility that awaits.

3. Nature's Artistry: Beauty Beyond Compare

As you set foot on Agios Sostis, nature's artistry unfolds before you in all its glory. The beach is a masterpiece of simplicity, with soft, golden sands that stretch gently along the shoreline. The crystal-clear waters of the Aegean lap at the coast, creating a soothing melody that accompanies your every step. Unlike some of the more commercialized beaches, Agios Sostis' natural beauty is unobstructed, allowing you to revel in the breathtaking views of the sea and the rolling hills beyond.

4. Secluded Tranquility and Relaxed Atmosphere

Agios Sostis stands as a retreat for those seeking respite from the world's chaos. Here, the absence of crowds and commercial distractions invites you to embrace the tranquility that defines the essence of the beach. The sound of the waves and the rustling of the sea breeze become your companions as you lounge on the sands, lost in the moment. It's a place where you can finally disconnect from the noise of modern life and reconnect with nature's soothing embrace.

5. Authentic Gastronomic Delights

Agios Sostis not only offers a feast for the soul but also for the senses. The beach is home to a charming taverna that captures the essence of Greek cuisine. The focus here is on authenticity and simplicity, with dishes made from locally sourced ingredients that highlight the flavors of the region. As you indulge in these culinary delights, you not only satisfy your taste buds but also contribute to the preservation of Agios Sostis' authentic charm.

6. An Oasis for Adventurous Souls

While Agios Sostis is a haven of relaxation, it also caters to the adventurous souls who seek exploration beyond the sands. The pristine waters beckon you to dive in and explore the underwater wonders that lie beneath the surface. Snorkeling reveals a world of marine life, from colorful fish to intricate coral formations. If you're feeling more adventurous, consider renting a kayak or a paddleboard to navigate the coast and discover hidden coves and rocky enclaves that are otherwise inaccessible.

7. Connecting with Nature's Rhythms

Agios Sostis offers more than just a picturesque view; it invites you to synchronize with the rhythms of nature. As the sun begins its descent, casting warm hues across the sky, and the sea mirrors its colors, you'll find yourself in a moment of perfect harmony with the world around you. Whether you're capturing the beauty through the lens of a camera or simply absorbing the scene with your senses, Agios Sostis gifts you with a connection to the universe's grandeur.

8. Tips for Embracing Agios Sostis' Tranquility

- Prepare for the Journey: Wear comfortable walking shoes, bring water, and be ready for a leisurely walk to the beach.
- Pack Thoughtfully: Keep your beach essentials simple; a towel, sunscreen, and a good book are often all you need.
- Arrive Early: To fully savor the serenity, consider visiting Agios Sostis early in the day to secure a prime spot.
- Respect Nature: As a secluded beach, Agios Sostis has minimal facilities. Leave no trace and respect the natural environment by taking your trash with you.

Agios Sostis stands as a testament to Mykonos' commitment to preserving its natural beauty amid a world of rapid development. Here, the simplicity of untouched landscapes coexists harmoniously with the serenity of the Aegean Sea. As you bid farewell to this secluded haven, carry with you the memory of its pristine allure, a reminder that even in a world of bustling progress, there are still places where time stands still and the beauty of nature reigns supreme.

Chapter 4

Mykonos Beyond the Shorelines

Unearth Delos Island's Ancient Secrets

A short distance from Mykonos, Delos Island serves as a reminder of a bygone past when mythology and history merge to form an archaeological marvel. Entering Delos' sacred territory is like entering a time machine that will transport you to a time when gods and people lived side by side, leaving behind a legacy that still fascinates modern explorers.

The Mythical Significance: A Divine Birthplace

At the heart of Delos' allure lies its legendary status as the birthplace of Apollo, the god of music, light, and prophecy, along with his twin sister Artemis, the goddess of the wilderness and the hunt. This sacred origin endowed Delos with profound religious importance in ancient Greece, making it a sanctuary of worship and a hub of cultural exchange.

Archaeological Marvels: Echoes of the Past

As you traverse the sprawling archaeological site of Delos, history comes alive through the remnants of grand temples, intricate mosaics, and marble statues that have defied the ages. The Terrace of the Lions, an iconic row of marble lion statues, stands proudly as a testament to the island's former magnificence, evoking awe and wonder.

House of Dionysus: A Glimpse into Ancient Lives

The House of Dionysus, an impeccably preserved dwelling on Delos, offers a glimpse into the daily lives of the island's inhabitants. Its exquisite mosaics narrate tales from Greek mythology, vividly illustrating the ancient stories that once captivated hearts and minds. These intricate artworks provide a tangible link to the artistic mastery of a bygone era.

The Sacred Lake: A Tranquil Sanctuary

At the heart of Delos lies a serene and mystical sacred lake. It was believed that Leto, the mother of Apollo and Artemis, gave birth to her divine offspring on its shores. The placid waters mirror the island's rich history, inviting visitors to contemplate the mystical connection between myth and reality.

Guided Tours and Interpretation: Delving Deeper

To fully unravel the historical tapestry of Delos, consider joining a guided tour. Expert guides unveil the layers of the island's past, offering insights into its mythological significance and archaeological wonders. Through their narratives, the stones and ruins come alive with stories of gods, mortals, and the eons that separated them.

Preservation Efforts: Guardians of History

Delos holds the prestigious designation of a UNESCO World Heritage Site, ensuring the preservation of its invaluable archaeological treasures. Visitors are entrusted with the responsibility of safeguarding this historical legacy by refraining from touching or removing artifacts. By respecting the island's past, we ensure its continued presence in the future.

Getting There: A Voyage to Remember

Embarking on the journey to Delos involves a short ferry ride from Mykonos. It's advisable to secure ferry tickets in advance, particularly during the bustling tourist seasons. As the ferry glides over the sparkling Aegean waters, the approach to Delos becomes an experience in itself, offering a foreshadowing of the captivating tales that await.

Reliving Ancient Epics

Unearthing the secrets of Delos is akin to walking through a portal to a time long past—a realm of gods, heroes, and legends. The island's archaeological riches, combined with its mythological legacy, create an immersive experience that transcends time. In the heart of the Aegean, Delos beckons travelers to delve into the narratives of antiquity, allowing history to unfold before their eyes, and myths to become tangible realities.

Ano Mera - Immerse in Traditional Village Life

Ano Mera, a captivating enclave nestled at the heart of Mykonos, stands as a testament to the island's rich cultural heritage. This section of the guide invites you to escape the lively beaches and bustling nightlife and step into the serene embrace of Ano Mera. Here, time slows down, offering a glimpse into the traditional Greek way of life.

Ano Mera: A Glimpse into Timeless Traditions

Ano Mera's Essence:
Ano Mera, nestled inland from the coastal allure, provides an authentic portrayal of Mykonos beyond the popular imagery. Cobblestone pathways wind their way through the village, flanked by white-washed houses adorned with vibrant splashes of bougainvillea. The

atmosphere exudes a sense of timelessness, where the charm of simplicity and community takes precedence.

The Monastery of Panagia Tourliani:
At the heart of Ano Mera stands the Monastery of Panagia Tourliani, an architectural marvel that serves as a historical anchor. This sanctuary, adorned with intricate marble work and a resplendent bell tower, encapsulates the island's spiritual significance. Within its walls, exquisite wooden iconostasis and frescoes narrate stories of faith and devotion that date back through generations.

Traditional Village Life:
A stroll through Ano Mera's narrow alleys is a journey back in time. Here, the rhythm of life is intertwined with traditions that have stood strong for centuries. Local tavernas, where homemade Greek delicacies are served with pride, create a sensory tapestry of tastes and aromas. Artisans crafting intricate pottery and textiles provide a

glimpse into crafts passed down through generations.

Experiencing Ano Mera

Panagia Tourliani Cultural Center:
The adjoining Panagia Tourliani Cultural Center serves as a bridge between past and present. Through exhibitions, interactive workshops, and live performances, visitors can delve deeper into Mykonos' cultural tapestry. Engaging with local artists and historians sheds light on the island's evolution and provides context to the traditions that endure.

Ano Mera Square:
Ano Mera's vibrant heart is its central square—a space pulsating with the collective energy of the community. Under the shade of ancient trees, locals and visitors converge to share stories, laughter, and life. The square hosts a dynamic medley of activities, from bustling markets adorned with local produce to joyous festivals celebrating traditions and heritage.

Agios Taxiarchis Church:

Ano Mera's spiritual resonance extends to the Agios Taxiarchis Church. This architectural jewel, with its characteristic blue dome, reflects the island's religious history. Inside, ornate details evoke a sense of reverence, while the views from the church offer panoramic vistas of the village and its surroundings, adding another layer to your experience.

Local Flavors and Traditions

Ano Mera's Culinary Delights:

The essence of Ano Mera's heritage is best savored through its culinary offerings. Local tavernas serve up a symphony of traditional Greek dishes, crafted with fresh, locally sourced ingredients. From the succulent flavors of grilled seafood to the heartwarming comfort of slow-cooked stews, each dish encapsulates generations of culinary mastery and community nourishment.

Cultural Celebrations:
If your visit coincides with local festivals, you're in for an immersive experience. Ano Mera's festive spirit comes alive during these occasions, painting the village with music, dance, and vibrant gatherings. Engaging in these celebrations not only provides insight into Mykonos' traditions but also offers an opportunity to forge connections with the island's heart and soul—its people.

Preserving Ano Mera's Legacy

Respecting Local Customs:
Ano Mera's authenticity is the result of its adherence to time-honored customs. When exploring the village, it's essential to approach the experience with respect for local traditions. This includes observing local norms, particularly when visiting places of worship, to ensure a harmonious interaction between visitors and the community.

Supporting Local Artisans:

The artisans of Ano Mera are the custodians of the village's cultural legacy. By engaging with their creations—whether it's purchasing handcrafted souvenirs or appreciating their craftsmanship—you contribute to the preservation of these traditions. Your support becomes a catalyst for the continuity of Mykonos' artistic heritage.

Ano Mera's Timeless Magic:

Ano Mera stands as a testament to the timelessness of Greece's cultural heritage. Through its streets, its people, and its traditions, this village imparts a profound understanding of a way of life that has stood resilient against the tides of change. As you traverse its pathways, interact with its inhabitants, and savor its flavors, you're transported to a place where the passage of time is marked by the echoes of tradition and the authenticity of human connection. Ano Mera, with its serene embrace, invites you to partake in the magic of Mykonos' cultural tapestry.

Sunset at Armenistis Lighthouse

A magnificent display is taking place at the Armenistis Lighthouse in Mykonos as the sun begins to set over the Aegean horizon. This famous landmark not only directs sailors but also invites tourists to witness a sunset that is just stunning. The Armenistis Lighthouse gives a vantage point that turns ordinary evenings into memorable ones. It is perched atop a rough hill overlooking the sea.

The Path Less Traveled: Journey to Armenistis Lighthouse

The journey to the Armenistis Lighthouse is an adventure in itself. Accessible by both road and foot, the lighthouse presents an opportunity to connect with Mykonos' natural beauty. For those who enjoy a stroll, a picturesque path meanders through the coastal landscape. As you walk, the invigorating sea breeze whispers secrets of the ocean, preparing you for the mesmerizing scene that awaits.

A Glimpse into Maritime History

Before immersing in the lighthouse's sunset charm, take a moment to appreciate its historical significance. The Armenistis Lighthouse has been a sentinel of the sea since 1891, guiding ships safely through Mykonos' waters. Its sturdy stone structure stands as a testament to the island's maritime heritage and the importance of this beacon to sailors of yesteryears.

Arrival at the Summit: Enchantment Awaits

As you ascend the hill to the lighthouse, anticipation builds. The panoramic view that gradually unfolds is truly awe-inspiring. Arriving at the summit, the deep blue of the Aegean stretches out before you, merging seamlessly with the sky. The lighthouse itself, a proud guardian of the coast, stands tall against this backdrop, offering the perfect contrast to nature's canvas.

The Dance of Colors: Sunset Splendor

As the sun begins its descent, a symphony of colors takes center stage. The clear azure sky gradually transforms into shades of gold, orange, and pink. The sea, reflecting the sky's palette, shimmers with ethereal brilliance. This is the moment that travelers and photographers alike eagerly await—a moment where time seems to slow, and the world is cast in the warm embrace of twilight.

Capturing the Moment: Photography Paradise

For photography enthusiasts, the Armenistis Lighthouse at sunset is a dream come true. The interplay of light and shadow, the silhouette of the lighthouse against the radiant sky, and the sea's gentle whispers all conspire to create a visual masterpiece. Whether using a professional camera or a smartphone, the memories captured here will undoubtedly become treasured keepsakes.

A Pause to Reflect: Contemplation and Tranquility

Beyond its visual splendor, the Armenistis Lighthouse offers a serene atmosphere conducive to reflection. As the sun dips below the horizon, there's an opportunity to contemplate the beauty of nature, the passage of time, and the role these timeless elements play in our lives. This sense of tranquility fosters a connection not only with the environment but also with oneself.

Local Insights and Legends: Stories of the Lighthouse

Engage with locals or guides, and you'll discover that the Armenistis Lighthouse holds more than just its physical beauty. Stories of maritime legends, historical events, and even myths enrich the experience. These narratives add depth to your visit, allowing you to appreciate the lighthouse's significance from both a cultural and a natural perspective.

A Memorable Evening: Departure with Awe and Gratitude

As the sun bids its final farewell, you'll likely find yourself lingering a little longer. The allure of the Armenistis Lighthouse at sunset is not easily forgotten. With the fading light, you'll begin your descent back to the world below. The memories of this magical evening, however, will accompany you, inspiring awe and gratitude for the simple yet profound beauty of nature and the human spirit.

In the heart of Mykonos, the Armenistis Lighthouse stands as a beacon not only for sailors but also for those seeking moments of transcendence. Its sunsets are a reminder that amid the rush of life, there exist pockets of time where the world takes on an otherworldly glow, and the soul finds solace in the embrace of nature's grandeur.

Culinary Delights: Enhancing the Experience

To enhance the magic of the Armenistis Lighthouse sunset, consider bringing a picnic or enjoying a meal from a local eatery. Sharing a meal against the backdrop of the setting sun adds an element of intimacy and indulgence to the experience. Imagine savoring the flavors of Greek cuisine while the sky undergoes its transformation—a sensory symphony that lingers in your memory long after you leave.

Timed to Perfection: Planning Your Visit

Timing is crucial when planning your visit to the Armenistis Lighthouse for sunset. To witness the full spectrum of colors and the lighthouse illuminated against the fading light, aim to arrive at least 30 minutes before the sun begins to set. This provides ample time to find a comfortable spot, set up your camera if you're photographing, and fully immerse in the experience.

Practical Tips for Visitors:
- Footwear: Wear comfortable shoes suitable for walking.
- Clothing: Bring a light jacket or shawl, as the evening breeze can be cool.
- Refreshments: Carry water and a light snack.
- Camera Equipment: If you're into photography, bring your camera, tripod, and any additional gear.
- Respect the Environment: Ensure you adhere to any local guidelines and regulations to preserve the natural beauty of the area.

A Personal Connection: Crafting Lasting Memories

Experiencing the sunset at the Armenistis Lighthouse goes beyond being a mere observer—it's about forming a personal connection with the surroundings. Whether you're sharing the moment with loved ones, documenting it through your lens, or simply allowing the experience to wash over you, the memory you carry will be uniquely your own.

A Symbol of Tranquility and Hope

The Armenistis Lighthouse, with its sentinel-like posture, represents more than just a navigational aid. It symbolizes a sense of security, a connection to the past, and a promise of new beginnings as the sun rises again. As you watch the sun dip below the horizon, you're reminded of the cyclical nature of life and the beauty that exists in embracing change.

A Farewell to the Day

As the sun's last rays kiss the sea, the Armenistis Lighthouse begins its watch over the night. The world around you gradually darkens, and the stars begin to twinkle in the sky. With a heart full of gratitude for the beauty witnessed, you'll descend the hill, leaving the lighthouse behind—its light a silent companion, guiding you back into the embrace of Mykonos' vibrant nightlife.

A Memory That Endures

The experience of witnessing the sunset at the Armenistis Lighthouse is more than a visual spectacle; it's a multi-sensory journey that resonates deep within. The interplay of light, the serenity of the sea, and the stories woven into the lighthouse's history create a memory that endures. When you close your eyes and recall that moment, you'll find yourself transported back to Mykonos—an island where time pauses, and the world is illuminated by the wonder of a setting sun.

Unraveling the Mystique of Ftelia Archaeological Site

The Ftelia Archaeological Site, a window into the island's ancient history, is tucked away along Mykonos' serene northern shore. This undiscovered treasure offers an astonishing excursion into the core of Mykonos' ancient history amid the vibrant beaches and busy town. Get ready to go inland as we set off on a journey of exploration into the mysterious kingdom of Ftelia.

1. A Glimpse into Ancient Life:
Transport yourself to a time when modernity was but a distant dream. Ftelia Archaeological Site dates back to the Neolithic era, around 5,000 BCE, making it a living testament to the enduring human presence on this captivating island. Here, you can wander amidst the remnants of dwellings, pathways, and artifacts

that once formed the fabric of everyday life for our forebears.

2. Archaeological Discoveries:
As you traverse the pathways of Ftelia, you'll find yourself amid an archaeological treasure trove. The meticulous excavations have unearthed an array of artifacts, each whispering tales of the past. Among the finds are pottery fragments, tools, and religious objects, each piece offering a tangible connection to the people who once called Ftelia home.

3. The Enigma of Prehistoric Ftelia:
Step into the shoes of ancient historians and ponder the mysteries that shroud Ftelia's past. Was it a trading hub, a seasonal settlement, or a spiritual haven? The riddle of its purpose continues to spark scholarly debate, adding to the allure of the site. As you explore, let your imagination roam and engage in the ongoing discourse that seeks to unravel Ftelia's secrets.

4. Exploring the Site:

Your journey at Ftelia Archaeological Site begins with the gentle crunch of gravel beneath your feet. As you walk through the site, you'll encounter remnants of ancient structures and pathways, leading you through a multi-layered narrative of Mykonos' evolution. Interpretive panels thoughtfully placed along the way offer insights into the historical context of the ruins that surround you.

5. Embracing the Atmosphere:

Beyond the physical remnants, Ftelia presents an emotional bridge to the past. Imagine the crackle of fires in the hearths, the laughter of families, and the communal activities that once animated these grounds. Stand amidst the foundations of ancient homes and let the whispers of bygone eras carry you to a different time.

6. Preservation and Education:

A vital part of your experience at Ftelia is contributing to its preservation. To ensure that this window into history remains open for future generations, treat the site with care and respect. Admire the artifacts from a respectful distance, resisting the urge to touch or disturb them. By doing so, you become a custodian of the past.

7. Planning Your Visit:
For a fulfilling visit to Ftelia Archaeological Site, consider these recommendations:
- Check Operating Hours: Ensure the site is open during your intended visit, as hours may vary.
- Guided Tours: Enhance your experience with a guided tour, where experts breathe life into the stories.
- Footwear and Attire: Opt for comfortable footwear suitable for uneven terrain, and dress according to the weather.
- Capturing Memories: Capture the essence of the site through photography, but remember to be mindful of its preservation.

8. Ftelia's Place in Modern Mykonos:
As you contemplate the ancient mysteries of Ftelia, take a moment to reflect on Mykonos'

dynamic evolution. This juxtaposition between antiquity and the island's modern vibrancy is a testament to Mykonos' ability to seamlessly weave the threads of history into its contemporary tapestry. Ftelia offers a rare opportunity to traverse the corridors of time and witness the dance of past and present.

Ftelia Archaeological Site transcends the sun-soaked beaches and the energetic town, beckoning you to embrace the legacy of Mykonos' ancestors. As you immerse yourself in the ruins, you'll unearth a deeper appreciation for the island's rich historical layers. Ftelia stands not only as a portal to Mykonos' past but also as a bridge that spans millennia, connecting the ancient whispers to the vibrant rhythm of today.

Horseback Riding and Rural Escapes

Venturing beyond the vibrant beaches and bustling promenades, Mykonos reveals another layer of its charm - a tranquil countryside and an invitation to experience it on horseback. This section unveils the peaceful allure of horseback riding and the quiet beauty of rural escapes, providing a unique perspective on Mykonos' lesser-explored dimensions.

Exploring the Countryside on Horseback: A Tranquil Journey:

Step away from the tourist hotspots and immerse yourself in the serene ambiance of Mykonos' hinterland. Horseback riding offers a chance to connect with the island's natural beauty at a leisurely pace. Guided tours, suitable for all skill levels, allow you to traverse hidden trails, meander through olive groves, and pass by traditional villages, immersing yourself in a world far removed from the glamorous beach scenes.

The Pleasures of Horseback Riding: Engaging with Nature:

As you mount your horse and embark on this unique adventure, you'll find that the rhythmic cadence of hooves against the earth harmonizes with the surroundings. The gentle sway as your horse moves forward, the rustle of leaves, and the scent of wildflowers create an immersive experience that brings you closer to nature. The expert guides accompanying you share insights into local flora, the history of the land, and anecdotes that infuse the journey with deeper meaning.

Scenic Routes and Enchanting Views: Captivating Perspectives:

Mykonos' diverse terrain lends itself to picturesque viewpoints that are best explored on horseback. Imagine cresting a hill to be greeted by panoramic vistas of the Aegean Sea stretching into the horizon. These breathtaking moments become indelible memories, capturing the island's beauty from a vantage point that words alone cannot convey. The sensation of being in harmony with the landscape while atop a horse creates an experience that's both tranquil and invigorating.

Rural Escapes: Unveiling Authentic Mykonos:

Venture into the heart of the island's authenticity with a visit to Ano Mera, a charming village that offers a glimpse of traditional Mykonos. Meander through its narrow streets lined with white-washed houses adorned with vibrant bougainvilleas. The centerpiece is the Monastery of Panagia Tourliani, a testament to the island's spiritual heritage. Engage with the locals, relish authentic Greek cuisine in local tavernas, and witness the rhythm of daily life that remains largely untouched by the glamour of the coast.

Escape to Agios Sostis: Tranquility by the Sea:

For those yearning for a secluded sanctuary, Agios Sostis awaits. This hidden gem, located on the northern coast, is devoid of the usual commercial developments. Unspoiled by crowds, Agios Sostis offers a stretch of beach hugged by rocky cliffs and embraced by crystalline waters. The absence of bustling beach bars makes it a tranquil retreat, a place to unwind and rejuvenate surrounded by nature's serenity.

Embrace the Rhythms of Mykonos' Countryside:

Horseback riding and rural escapes offer a symphony of sensations that blend equine companionship, the quietude of nature, and the authenticity of village life. They provide an avenue to experience a different facet of Mykonos—one where the pace slows down, and the soul of the island is revealed. Whether you're an equestrian enthusiast or a novice, these experiences deliver a genuine connection to Mykonos' rural heart.

A Journey Beyond the Ordinary:

In the realm of horseback riding and rural exploration, Mykonos opens its heart to those who seek a deeper understanding of its character. As you journey through ancient paths, connect with local guides, and immerse yourself in the island's rustic beauty, you'll uncover an aspect of Mykonos that's seldom experienced. These moments emphasize that Mykonos isn't solely about beaches; it's an island woven with narratives, traditions, and breathtaking vistas that extend well beyond the coastline. Saddle up and embark on this remarkable voyage—a journey through the unspoiled heartland of Mykonos.

Chapter 5

Crafting Unforgettable 2023 Experiences

Mykonos Nightlife - Epic Parties and Entertainment

When the sun slips beneath the Aegean horizon, Mykonos undergoes a metamorphosis into a realm of pulsating beats, dazzling lights, and unbridled revelry. The island's nightlife in 2023 promises an evolution of exhilarating experiences that cater to all tastes, from beachside extravaganzas to enchanting town soirées.

1. The Legendary Beach Clubs: Where Day Turns into Night
The beaches of Mykonos are not merely for lazing about throughout the day. The beach clubs adopt a different identity when dusk falls. Imagine visiting Scorpios, which is tucked away

on Paraga Beach. An all-encompassing sensory experience is characteristic of this famous location. In 2023, Scorpios become even more alluring by throwing well-designed amenities that synchronize music, art, and cuisine. Enjoy masterfully made drinks while relaxing next to a turquoise pool and soaking in breath-blowing sea views. An additional highlight of Mykonos' nightlife is the Nammos Beach Club on Psarou Beach. With oceanfront cabanas, champagne sprays, and live performances by worldwide musicians, this year's edition is intended to redefine opulence.

2. The Enigmatic Mykonos Town: Winding Streets to Neon Lights

Mykonos Town, known as Chora, transforms from a charming labyrinth of whitewashed buildings by day into a labyrinth of vibrant energy by night. Begin your evening at the iconic windmills – a testament to the island's history. Then, meander through narrow alleys where boutiques and art galleries beckon. As darkness falls, the streets come alive with the buzz of nightlife. Galleraki Cocktail Bar, a local gem, invites you to unwind with a selection of cocktails that mirror the kaleidoscope of emotions found on the island. Scarpa Bar offers an intimate setting, where mixologists craft concoctions inspired by Mykonos' unique character.

3. Sunset Champagne Cruises: An Unforgettable Prelude

The transition from day to night on Mykonos is as mesmerizing as its nightlife. Consider embarking on a sunset champagne cruise. Picture yourself on the deck of a luxury yacht, the sun casting its golden hues on the crystal waters. The clinking of glasses mingles with laughter as you toast to the Aegean's breathtaking beauty. As the sun dips below the horizon, you'll witness a spectacle that ignites the night to come.

4. Dance into the Wee Hours: Clubs that Define the Night

Mykonos' reputation as a party haven is anchored by its electrifying clubs, and 2023 promises an even more pulsating beat. Cavo Paradiso, poised on a cliff, offers panoramic views of the sea and dance floors that transform into arenas of euphoria. Internationally acclaimed DJs ignite nights with music that traverses genres. The Paradise Club, nestled by the sea, continues its legacy with its expansive dance floors and its diverse roster of artists. This year, expect thematic nights that transport you to different eras, enhancing the immersive experience.

5. Themed Extravaganzas and Immersive Performances

Mykonos' nightlife in 2023 is an evolution beyond music; it's a canvas of creativity and expression. Themed parties have taken on a new dimension, inviting you to dive into different worlds. Engage in the glamor of retro '80s nights or the whimsy of Bohemian extravaganzas. Beyond the music, expect immersive performances that merge art, music, and technology. Witness avant-garde shows that challenge the conventional nightclub experience and blur the lines between reality and artistry.

6. Mykonos After Dark: A Wholesome Mix of Tastes

Beyond the dance floors and extravagant parties, Mykonos' nightlife offers quieter yet equally enriching experiences. Wine aficionados will find themselves at home at Notos Exclusive Wine Bar & Restaurant, an establishment that boasts an extensive collection of Greek and international wines. Scarpa Wine, tucked into a charming courtyard, offers a selection that resonates with the island's essence. Here, you can savor fine wines under the open sky, engaging in conversations that meander like the streets of Mykonos Town.

Mykonos' nightlife in 2023 transcends the ordinary, inviting you to partake in a spectrum of experiences that range from dance-floor euphoria to intimate conversations under the stars. Whether you're amid the beach club extravagance, embracing the mystique of Mykonos Town, or savoring wine in tranquil settings, the island's nightlife promises unforgettable memories. As the night enfolds you in its allure, prepare to dance, revel, and forge connections that will linger long after the music fades.

Yachting and Sailing: Aegean Dreams Set Sail

Venturing into the open waters around Mykonos is a transformative experience, one that carries you away on the gentle waves of the Aegean Sea. In this section, we'll immerse ourselves in the world of yachting and sailing, exploring the luxury of yachting charters and the exhilaration of setting sail on a personal journey.

Yachting: Luxury on the Aegean Waves

Indulge in the Ultimate Experience:
When it comes to experiencing Mykonos from the sea, luxury yacht charters offer an unparalleled way to bask in opulence. Picture yourself stepping aboard a sleek, private yacht—a floating haven of comfort and extravagance. Many yacht charters in Mykonos come complete with a professional crew, including a captain, chef, and attentive staff, all

dedicated to making your voyage seamless and delightful.

Seamless Sophistication:
The allure of yachting lies in the seamless sophistication it provides. Set sail from Mykonos' shores, and you'll find yourself embraced by the tranquil beauty of the Aegean. Lounge on the expansive decks, where the sun's gentle caress is accompanied by breathtaking views. Savor gourmet meals, artfully crafted onboard by skilled chefs, and savor the sensation of being completely at ease in a world defined by luxury.

Personalized Itineraries:
One of the many draws of yachting in Mykonos is the ability to tailor your journey to your preferences. Whether you're drawn to lively beach parties or serene hideaways, there's an itinerary that caters to your desires. Seek out the romantic solitude of Rineia Island or drop anchor near the iconic Super Paradise Beach,

where the vibrant party scene unfurls along the shoreline.

Sailing: Navigating the Aegean Breez

Unleash Your Inner Sailor:
For those who seek an immersive adventure, sailing offers the opportunity to be an active participant in your voyage. Step aboard a catamaran or monohull yacht and become a vital part of the crew. Feel the exhilaration as you lend a hand in raising the sails, take the helm, and navigate the vessel through the open waters. The Aegean breeze fills the sails, propelling you forward, and the connection between you, the yacht, and the sea becomes a palpable and exhilarating reality.

Sail to Hidden Gems:
Sailing offers a unique advantage—the freedom to explore lesser-known destinations that larger vessels may not reach. Venture to secluded coves, anchor in hidden bays, and uncover the untouched beauty that Mykonos has to offer.

From the pristine sands of Agios Sostis to the captivating village of Fokos, sailing promises discovery beyond the beaten path.

Navigational Tips and Considerations

Choosing the Right Charter:
Selecting the perfect yacht charter involves aligning your preferences with the charter's offerings. Luxury charters provide an extravagance-filled journey, while bareboat charters cater to those who wish to take an active role in sailing. Research different charter companies, delve into customer reviews, and communicate your desires to ensure your chosen charter aligns seamlessly with your expectations.

Timing Matters:
Understanding the ideal time to embark on a yachting or sailing adventure in Mykonos is paramount. The island's peak tourist season, stretching from May to September boasts ideal weather conditions—warm temperatures, calm seas, and gentle winds. To relish a more serene

experience, consider visiting during shoulder seasons like May-June or September, where fewer crowds enhance your maritime escapades.

Respect the Environment:
As you embrace the Aegean, remember the responsibility to safeguard its delicate ecosystem. Refrain from anchoring in protected areas and fragile marine environments. Adopt eco-friendly practices such as refraining from feeding marine life, minimizing waste production, and utilizing biodegradable products to ensure that the stunning waters of Mykonos remain pristine for generations to come.

Local Insights:
Engaging with locals and the knowledgeable crew on your yacht can provide invaluable insights. Seek recommendations for hidden gems, lesser-known diving spots, and the most picturesque places to drop anchor. Their expertise enhances your experience, enabling you to engage with Mykonos on a more profound level and uncover its authentic essence.

In 2023, the world of yachting and sailing in Mykonos is a gateway to exploration and connection—both with the stunning landscapes and the sea's timeless rhythm. Whether you opt for the lavish luxury of a yacht charter or the hands-on adventure of sailing, the Aegean waves will be your guide, and the beauty of Mykonos will become an integral part of your journey. So, embark on this maritime odyssey, embrace the salty breeze, and let the allure of Mykonos unfold before your eyes, creating memories that will last a lifetime.

Culinary Journeys: Greek Delights and Gourmet Feasts

In the heart of Mykonos' enchantment lies a gastronomic odyssey that tantalizes the senses and captures the essence of Greek cuisine. Section 3 of Chapter 5 delves into the culinary landscape of Mykonos, where every dish is a celebration of tradition, flavor, and creativity. From traditional tavernas to upscale dining establishments, Mykonos offers a palate-pleasing adventure that reflects its rich history and modern vibrancy.

1. A Taste of Tradition: Greek Cuisine Beyond Borders

Immerse yourself in the culinary heritage of Greece, where the Mediterranean flavors take center stage. Mykonos' dining scene proudly showcases traditional Greek dishes prepared with locally sourced ingredients, delivering an authentic and memorable dining experience.

1.1 A Mezze Feast: Sharing and Savoring

Embark on a journey of shared indulgence with mezze, a collection of small, flavorful dishes that evoke the essence of Greek culture. From creamy tzatziki and hummus to crispy spanakopita and savory dolmades, each bite narrates tales of generations past. Sit by the sea at a taverna and savor the art of conversation over a spread of mezze, perfectly paired with local wines.

The tradition of mezze goes beyond mere sustenance; it's a way of life. Engage in the art of togetherness as you share a platter of olives, feta cheese, and sun-drenched tomatoes. The communal aspect of mezze dining fosters a sense of camaraderie and warmth, echoing the heartwarming hospitality of the Greek people.

1.2 Seafood Symphony: Fresh Catches of the Day

Mykonos' proximity to the sea gifts its cuisine with an abundance of fresh seafood. Dive into an array of dishes featuring octopus, grilled fish, calamari, and succulent prawns. Experience the essence of Mykonos' maritime life as you dine overlooking the glistening Aegean waters.

The azure waters surrounding Mykonos provide a bounty of seafood that's woven into the island's culinary fabric. Imagine savoring a plate of tender octopus, grilled to perfection and drizzled with a zesty lemon dressing. The seafood symphony extends beyond taste; it's a visual feast that echoes the island's natural beauty.

2. Elevating Greek Gastronomy: Gourmet Dining with a Mykonian Twist

Mykonos doesn't just celebrate tradition; it also embraces innovation. This subsection explores the upscale dining establishments that are redefining Greek cuisine, blending tradition with contemporary culinary artistry.

2.1 Fusion of Flavors: Creative Interpretations

Experience the works of visionary chefs who take Greek classics and infuse them with modern techniques and global influences. Dine on dishes that transform moussaka into a culinary masterpiece and reimagine baklava as a deconstructed dessert. Allow your taste buds to explore new horizons while staying true to the roots of Greek cuisine.

At Mykonos' upscale eateries, the culinary journey becomes an adventure of the senses. Picture a plate where traditional moussaka is deconstructed into layers of flavor, artfully plated to delight the eyes before the taste buds. The chefs' creativity knows no bounds, presenting Greek cuisine as an evolving narrative that pays homage to the past while embracing the future.

2.2 Farm-to-Table Delights: Local Ingredients, Exquisite Dishes

Savor the terroir of Mykonos through farm-to-table dining experiences that celebrate the island's agricultural bounty. Explore menus featuring organic vegetables, artisanal cheeses, and aromatic herbs grown on the island. Indulge in dishes that showcase the purity of flavors and the dedication of local producers.

Farm-to-table dining on Mykonos is an homage to the land's generosity. Imagine savoring a salad composed of sun-ripened tomatoes, crisp cucumbers, and hand-picked olives, all sourced from local farms. The commitment to sustainability and local produce not only enhances the flavor but also fosters a deep connection with the land and its people.

3. Sweet Temptations: Desserts that Whisper Mykonian Stories

No culinary journey is complete without indulging in the sweet offerings that grace

Mykonos' tables. Discover the captivating world of Mykonian desserts, where every bite tells a tale of tradition, love, and celebration.

3.1 Divine Nectar: Loukoumades and Honey Delights

Treat yourself to loukoumades, heavenly Greek doughnuts drizzled with golden honey and sprinkled with crushed nuts. These bite-sized delights are a taste of pure indulgence, reminiscent of the island's joyous festivals and gatherings.

In every bite of loukoumades, the sweetness of honey mingles with the delicate crunch of nuts, transporting you to the heart of Mykonos' celebratory spirit. Imagine enjoying these treats by the waterfront, the sound of waves harmonizing with the laughter of fellow diners.

3.2 Island Elegance: The Art of Pasteli

Uncover the art of pasteli, a sweet confection made from sesame seeds and honey. Experience a culinary masterpiece that encapsulates the essence of Mykonos' simplicity and elegance, offering a glimpse into the island's artisanal heritage.

Pasteli is more than a dessert; it's a symbol of Mykonos' dedication to craftsmanship. Picture the process of crafting pasteli, where golden honey and sesame seeds are meticulously combined to create a delicate balance of sweetness and nuttiness. Each bite is a tribute to the island's artisanal legacy, an expression of beauty in simplicity.

4. Wine and Dine: Exploring Mykonos' Oenological Charms

In this subsection, we raise a toast to Mykonos' oenological treasures. From local wineries to wine bars, immerse yourself in the island's burgeoning wine culture that complements its culinary delights.

4.1 Vineyard Adventures: Unveiling Mykonos' Terroir

Embark on vineyard tours that reveal the secrets of Mykonos' wine production. Explore the island's unique grape varietals and learn about the wine-making process that results in distinctive and delightful flavors.

Walking through the lush vineyards of Mykonos, you'll witness the synergy between the land and the vines. Imagine the scent of sun-kissed grapes filling the air as the winemaker shares stories of the island's viticultural heritage. Engage in the grape-harvesting process, picking ripe clusters that will later transform into the nectar of Mykonos. As you savor each sip of wine, you'll taste the dedication of local vintners to preserving the island's terroir.

4.2 Wine Bars and Tastings: Sip and Savor

Delight in the ambiance of Mykonos' charming wine bars, where sommeliers guide you through tastings of local wines. Experience the harmonious interplay of wine and cuisine as you pair each glass with dishes that elevate the tasting experience.

Imagine the warm glow of a candle-lit wine bar, where you're introduced to Mykonos' oenological secrets. Sip on a glass of crisp Assyrtiko, a local white wine, and feel its citrusy notes dance on your palate. Pair it with a plate of grilled octopus drizzled with olive oil and sprinkled with herbs—a symphony of flavors that accentuate the nuances of both wine and food.

A Culinary Journey to Remember

As you conclude your culinary journey through Mykonos, you'll carry with you the flavors, aromas, and stories that define Greek cuisine on this enchanting island. From humble tavernas to innovative dining establishments, Mykonos offers an alluring fusion of tradition and innovation that captivates every traveler's taste buds. Savor the memories of each dish and every sip, and let Mykonos' culinary tapestry remain a cherished part of your journey through the Aegean paradise.

Indulge in the heritage of mezze, seafood feasts, and innovative culinary creations that infuse Greek cuisine with modern flair. Delight in the artistry of traditional desserts and the elegance of pasteli. Raise a glass to Mykonos' flourishing wine culture, where vineyard explorations and wine tastings enhance your journey. Your culinary voyage through Mykonos reveals a tapestry of tastes that beautifully weaves together tradition, innovation, and the island's rich culture.

Mykonos Shopping: A Fusion of Tradition and Modernity

Mykonos' Markets and Boutiques: As you stroll through the enchanting streets of Mykonos Town, you'll find yourself immersed in a world of markets and boutiques that beckon with their vibrant displays. Matoyianni Street stands as the bustling heart of shopping in Chora, offering an array of boutique shops that span the spectrum from high-end fashion and exquisite jewelry to exquisite homeware and meticulously crafted handicrafts. The juxtaposition of the traditional Cycladic architecture and the modern storefronts creates an ambiance that is uniquely Mykonian, inviting you to explore and discover.

Captivating Souvenirs: The act of shopping in Mykonos is not merely a transaction; it's an opportunity to encapsulate the essence of the island in your purchases. Mykonos' souvenir shops are veritable treasure troves of cultural representation. Amidst these stalls, you'll find intricately designed evil eye talismans that symbolize protection and good fortune, allowing you to carry a piece of the island's spiritual beliefs with you. Hand-painted ceramics, vibrant textiles, and delicate lacework stand as more than just mementos – they embody the island's artistic heritage, a snapshot of its intricate tapestry.

Discovering Local Artistry

Art Galleries and Studios: Mykonos' creative spirit finds its expression in a myriad of art galleries and studios scattered across the island. These spaces provide a glimpse into the contemporary art scene that is thriving on this historical island. Galleries such as Rarity Gallery and The House of Fine Art (HOFA) offer an eclectic mix of artistic styles, showcasing the works of both local talents and international artists. The exhibitions and installations are windows into the island's cultural evolution, providing an opportunity to engage with art that reflects the fusion of Mykonos' rich history and its ever-evolving identity.

Jewelry and Fashion: Mykonos' jewelry designers and fashion boutiques harmoniously blend traditional craftsmanship with modern aesthetics, resulting in pieces that are not just ornaments but stories in metal and fabric. The island's jewelry designers draw inspiration from the vivid natural landscapes and the mythology that surrounds Mykonos. The intricate designs, often reminiscent of the sea's undulating waves and the island's whitewashed charm, add an extra layer of significance to the pieces. Similarly, the island's fashion boutiques offer bespoke clothing that effortlessly combines traditional motifs with contemporary flair, allowing you to carry a piece of Mykonos' style with you.

Local Crafts and Workshops

Traditional Craftsmanship: Mykonos' vibrant artisanal heritage is a testament to the skills that have been passed down through generations. Visiting workshops that specialize in traditional crafts provides an intimate look at the island's artisanal legacy. Witnessing skilled artisans meticulously creating intricate lacework known as "panel" or "kladisma" and handweaving baskets from natural materials allows you to appreciate the dedication and artistry that goes into each piece. These workshops become not just shopping destinations but immersive experiences that connect you with the island's cultural roots.

Interactive Experiences: Some of Mykonos' workshops offer immersive experiences that allow you to become a part of the creative process. Participate in pottery classes, where you'll learn to mold and shape clay into beautiful creations, all while guided by skilled professionals. Alternatively, engage in jewelry-making workshops, where you can craft your unique pieces under the guidance of local experts. These interactive experiences provide you with not only a tangible souvenir but also cherished memories of your creative endeavors on the island.

Culinary Souvenirs

Flavors of Mykonos: Mykonos' culinary scene isn't confined to its restaurants; it extends to its culinary souvenirs, allowing you to take the island's flavors home with you. Discover local food products that encapsulate Mykonos' rich gastronomic heritage. Aromatic spices, organic olive oil, and aged wines are just a few examples of the edible treasures that await. Delve into traditional sweets like "amygdalota" (almond cookies) and "melopita" (honey pie) that encapsulate the island's sweet traditions, offering you a taste of Mykonos' culinary tapestry.

Cooking Workshops: To deepen your connection with Mykonian gastronomy, consider participating in cooking workshops. These workshops not only provide you with the opportunity to learn to prepare authentic island dishes but also allow you to become a part of the island's culinary narrative. Master the art of making "kopanisti," a flavorful local cheese spread, or try your hand at crafting the iconic Greek "loukoumades" (honey balls). As you engage in these workshops, you're not just acquiring culinary skills; you're immersing yourself in the island's flavors and traditions.

Sustainability and Responsible Shopping

Supporting Local Communities: Shopping in Mykonos goes beyond the acquisition of material goods; it's an opportunity to support local communities and preserve traditional skills. Many of Mykonos' artisans and craftsmen are deeply intertwined with the local fabric, and by purchasing their products, you're directly contributing to their livelihoods and the continuation of their artistry. Your shopping choices become a means of sustaining the island's cultural heritage, ensuring that the skills and traditions are passed down to future generations.

Eco-Friendly Souvenirs: Embrace responsible shopping by seeking out eco-friendly souvenirs that align with Mykonos' commitment to environmental consciousness. Many of the island's artisans and designers are conscious of sustainability, crafting items from recycled materials or sustainable resources. By choosing such souvenirs, you not only bring home a tangible piece of Mykonos but also leave a positive impact on the island's delicate ecosystem, contributing to its long-term preservation.

Mykonos shopping is an adventure of discovery and immersion, where every purchase tells a story and every item encapsulates the island's history, creativity, and vibrancy. From the bustling markets of Mykonos Town to the intimate workshops where artisans craft intricate lacework, the island's shopping experiences are an invitation to become a part of its narrative. As you explore the galleries, boutiques, and markets, you're not just acquiring souvenirs; you're embracing the culture and soul of

Mykonos. These cherished keepsakes will continue to resonate with you, serving as tangible memories that bring you back to the enchanting island again and again.

Retreat to Wellness: Spa Escapes and Rejuvenation

Amidst the vibrant rhythms of Mykonos, a haven of tranquility awaits those in search of solace and revitalization. In the depth of Section 5, we embark on a journey into the serene realm of Mykonos' wellness landscape, where spa escapes beckon to soothe both body and spirit.

5.1 The Art of Mykonos Wellness: Nurturing the Soul and Body

Stepping beyond Mykonos' glittering facade reveals a world deeply attuned to the art of wellness. Amidst the island's dynamic pulse, the wellness scene stands as a testament to the island's commitment to holistic rejuvenation. Amidst the bustling streets and sandy shores, Mykonos offers a range of luxurious spa retreats and centers, designed to harmonize the body and mind, embracing both ancient Grecian wisdom and contemporary wellness techniques.

5.2 Mykonos Spa Escapes: A Symphony of Rejuvenation

Close your eyes and envision yourself cocooned in a world of opulent pampering, where the worries of life recede like distant echoes. From lavish resort sanctuaries to intimate boutique retreats, Mykonos unfurls an array of choices, each offering its unique tapestry of wellness. With the Aegean breeze as a gentle backdrop, spa escapes in Mykonos promise to transport you into a realm of serene relaxation, where the touch of skilled therapists guides you on a transformative journey.

5.3 Ancient Wisdom Meets Modern Techniques: A Fusion of Healing Traditions

Within Mykonos' embrace, the threads of history intertwine with modern practices, creating a tapestry of wellness that's as rooted in tradition as it is contemporary. Experience treatments inspired by the tales of ancient Greece, where ingredients like golden olive oil, soothing honey, and fragrant herbs become tools of rejuvenation. Through massages that revive, facials that invigorate, and therapies that honor the island's heritage, Mykonos infuses age-old practices with the vigor of modern wellness trends.

5.4 Wellness by the Sea: Nourishing the Senses

Mykonos' connection to the sea is a defining aspect of its wellness narrative. Picture yourself basking in open-air massages, the rhythmic ebb and flow of the waves acting as a calming cadence. Engage in invigorating yoga sessions on secluded beaches, where the expansive horizon becomes a canvas for meditation. The healing embrace of the sea weaves its magic into therapies, fostering an intimate dialogue between nature and well-being.

5.5 Mind, Body, and Soul Reconnection: A Holistic Retreat

Beyond mere physical rejuvenation, Mykonos' wellness ethos delves into the deeper realms of the mind, body, and soul. Embark on holistic wellness journeys that invite you to explore mindfulness through meditation, partake in transformative workshops, and embrace the island's peaceful environs. These immersive experiences foster a profound connection with yourself and the island's natural beauty, leaving you with a sense of balance and renewal that transcends the surface.

5.6 Tailored Experiences for Every Visitor: Your Wellness Journey

Mykonos' wellness offerings stand as a testament to the island's commitment to individuality. Whatever your wellness aspirations—be it relaxation, detoxification, or rejuvenation—Mykonos offers an array of experiences that cater to your unique needs.

From day-long wellness retreats to comprehensive multi-day escapes, Mykonos ensures that your journey toward well-being is a personalized and transformative one.

5.7 Bringing Mykonos Wellness Home: Souvenirs of Serenity

As you bid farewell to Mykonos, you need not leave behind the essence of its rejuvenating embrace. Many of the island's wellness havens extend their offerings to wellness products inspired by indigenous ingredients. These souvenirs—ranging from indulgent skincare products to aromatic oils—serve as tangible tokens of your tranquil moments on this enchanting island, allowing you to carry Mykonos' healing spirit wherever your adventures lead.

The Harmonious Melody of Renewal

Amidst the vivacious pulse of Mykonos, Section 5 has unveiled the sanctuary of wellness, inviting you to seek solace and renewal amidst the island's energetic embrace. Here, ancient traditions seamlessly meld with contemporary practices, offering you a symphony of rejuvenation. From open-air massages by the sea to immersive holistic workshops, Mykonos' wellness scene invites you to savor the gift of restoration. As you emerge refreshed and rejuvenated, you're poised to continue your exploration of the island's myriad wonders, carrying with you the harmonious melody of renewal.

Chapter 6:

Celebrate Summer in Mykonos

Mykonos' Cultural Feast: Festivals and Events

Mykonos is not only a place of stunning beaches and vibrant nightlife; it's also a cultural hub that comes alive with a rich tapestry of festivals and events during the summer months. Immerse yourself in the island's local traditions, music, and arts, and discover the unique experiences that these celebrations bring to your Mykonos journey.

1.1 The Essence of Mykonos' Cultural Calendar

The summer months in Mykonos are marked by a series of captivating festivals and events that pay homage to the island's history, heritage, and vibrant present. From traditional religious celebrations to modern music festivals, the island hosts a diverse range of gatherings that draw both locals and visitors into their lively embrace.

1.2 Panigiria: Traditional Religious Festivals

Panigiria, or traditional Greek festivals, are a window into Mykonos' rich cultural heritage. These events are deeply rooted in local traditions and often honor a patron saint or historical figure. One of the most notable panegyric is the Feast of Agios Ioannis (Saint John), the island's patron saint, celebrated on August 29th. The festival includes processions, live music, traditional dancing, and a sense of camaraderie that brings the community together.

1.3 Music and Arts Festivals: Mykonos Unplugged

Mykonos' cultural scene is vibrant, and during the summer, the island becomes a haven for music and art enthusiasts. The Mykonos Music Festival, held at various venues across the island, showcases a mix of classical, jazz, and contemporary music, attracting international and local talents alike. Art exhibitions and gallery openings also abound during this season, providing a platform for artists to showcase their creativity in a picturesque setting.

1.4 The Mykonos Biennale: A Fusion of Art and Culture

For those seeking a deeper connection to Mykonos' cultural tapestry, the Mykonos Biennale is a must-attend event. Held every odd-numbered year, this international arts festival is a celebration of contemporary art, performances, and creative dialogues. The festival's immersive experiences often blur the lines between art and reality, allowing participants to engage with thought-provoking installations and interact with artists from around the world.

1.5 Dance to the Rhythm: Folklore and Music

Music and dance are integral to Mykonian culture, and various events spotlight these traditional forms of expression. The "Mykonos Dances" festival showcases local dance groups, preserving age-old choreographies and costumes. This event is a testament to the islanders' commitment to passing down their cultural heritage to younger generations.

1.6 Participate and Connect: Local Workshops

Many festivals in Mykonos offer workshops that provide a hands-on experience of the island's cultural elements. Engage in traditional Greek cooking classes, learn to dance the syrtaki, or try your hand at pottery. These workshops not only allow you to learn new skills but also provide a deeper understanding of the island's culture and traditions.

1.7 Embrace the Local Spirit

Immersing yourself in Mykonos' cultural festivals and events offers more than just entertainment; it's an opportunity to connect with the island on a profound level. Whether you're joining a lively dance, savoring traditional cuisine, or simply enjoying the vibrant atmosphere, these celebrations provide a glimpse into the heart and soul of Mykonos.

1.8 Planning Your Festival Experience

Before your trip to Mykonos, research the festivals and events scheduled during your visit. Many festivals have specific dates, so plan your itinerary accordingly. Check for any entrance fees, ticket availability, and special activities that you might want to participate in. Embrace the local spirit, open yourself to new experiences, and celebrate Mykonos' culture with fellow travelers and islanders alike.

In the cultural melting pot that is Mykonos, festivals and events are more than occasions to celebrate; they are gateways to understanding the island's history, traditions, and contemporary creativity. Immerse yourself in the local culture, dance to the rhythms, and engage with the island's vibrant spirit. Mykonos' festivals offer an unforgettable dimension to your journey, leaving you with memories that will last a lifetime.

1.9 Embrace the Night: Mykonos' Nighttime Cultural Scene

As the sun sets over Mykonos, the island transforms into a nocturnal wonderland where cultural experiences continue to flourish. The streets come alive with the sounds of music, the aromas of delicious cuisine, and the energy of people gathering to celebrate life.

1.10 Music and Entertainment Venues

Mykonos boasts an array of music and entertainment venues that offer a diverse range of performances. From traditional Greek music to international DJs spinning the latest beats, you'll find something to suit your musical tastes. The intimate settings of many venues create an atmosphere that fosters a deep connection between performers and the audience.

1.11 Dance the Night Away: Traditional Greek Dances

In Mykonos, dance is a universal language that brings people together. Many bars and tavernas host Greek dance nights, where both locals and visitors can join in the festivities. Dance instructors often guide participants through traditional steps, allowing them to immerse themselves in the rhythmic culture of Greece.

1.12 The Joy of Greek Cuisine: Food and Music Festivals

Mykonos' vibrant food scene is often accompanied by live music, especially during food and wine festivals. These festivals offer a unique opportunity to sample local delicacies while enjoying live performances by Greek musicians. The combination of flavors and melodies creates an unforgettable sensory experience.

1.13 Cultural Dialogues: Artist Talks and Exhibitions

Art and culture collide during artist talks and exhibitions hosted in various venues across the island. Engage with artists, photographers, and creators who share their inspiration, creative processes, and insights. These events provide a unique perspective on Mykonos' artistic landscape and offer a chance to connect with like-minded individuals.

1.14 Planning Your Nighttime Cultural Adventures

To fully embrace Mykonos' nighttime cultural scene, plan your evenings wisely. Research local events, performances, and venues that align with your interests. Consider joining group activities like dance classes or art workshops to engage in meaningful cultural experiences. Be open to mingling with fellow travelers and locals, as these interactions often lead to memorable connections and shared adventures.

1.15 Embracing Mykonos' Cultural Diversity

What makes Mykonos' cultural celebrations truly special is the island's ability to seamlessly blend traditional and contemporary elements. As you navigate the festivals and events, you'll witness the convergence of ancient traditions with modern creativity. This fusion is a testament to Mykonos' dynamic spirit and its dedication to preserving its heritage while embracing the present.

1.16 A Lasting Impression

As you immerse yourself in Mykonos' cultural festivals and nighttiscenesene, you'll leave with more than just memories. You'll carry with you a deeper understanding of the island's soul, its history, and the people who call it home. Mykonos' cultural celebrations offer a unique perspective, a chance to connect, and an invitation to dance, sing, and celebrate under the starlit Aegean sky.

1.17 Capturing the Magic

Don't forget to capture the magic of Mykonos' cultural celebrations through photos and journals. Document your experiences, the people you meet, and the moments that resonate with you. These keepsakes will serve as a cherished reminder of your journey into Mykonos' cultural heart.

1.18 The Journey Continues

As you explore Mykonos' cultural festivals and events, remember that the journey is ongoing. Each festival, dance, and celebration is an invitation to delve deeper into the island's vibrant culture. Keep an open heart and an adventurous spirit, and let Mykonos' cultural allure guide you to new and meaningful encounters throughout your stay.

In the heart of Mykonos, the nights come alive with a symphony of cultural experiences. From traditional dance to modern music, from local cuisine to contemporary art, the island's nocturnal scene invites you to be part of its ongoing story. So, join the festivities, dance to the rhythms, and create memories that will forever be intertwined with the spirit of Mykonos.

1.19 Insider Tips for a Memorable Nighttime Cultural Experience

To make the most of Mykonos' nighttime cultural scene, consider these insider tips:

- Plan Ahead: Research local events and venues before your trip. Check out event schedules, performances, and workshops that align with your interests.

- Local Recommendations: Don't hesitate to ask locals for their recommendations. They often have insights into hidden gems and lesser-known events that offer authentic cultural experiences.

- Dress the Part: Depending on the event, consider dressing in attire that aligns with the theme. Whether it's traditional Greek clothing or chic island style, embracing the dress code can enhance your immersion in the experience.

- Arrive Early: Arriving early at events allows you to secure a good spot and interact with performers and fellow attendees before the festivities begin.

- Engage with Others: Cultural celebrations are a fantastic opportunity to connect with both locals and travelers. Strike up conversations, share stories, and make new friends who share your enthusiasm for culture and exploration.

- Capture the Moments: Keep your camera or smartphone handy to capture the vibrant energy of the cultural celebrations. Photographs and videos will help you relive the magic long after the event ends.

- Respect Local Customs: While you're celebrating, remember to respect local customs and traditions. Pay attention to any guidelines or etiquette specific to the event.

- Savor the Flavors: Many cultural events include traditional food and beverages. Take the opportunity to savor local delicacies and enjoy the unique flavors of Mykonos.

- Be Open to Surprises: Sometimes the most memorable moments come from unexpected encounters. Be open to going with the flow and embracing the spontaneity of cultural celebrations.

1.20 Taking the Spirit of Mykonos Home with You

As you partake in Mykonos' cultural festivities and embrace its nighttime cultural scene, consider how you can carry the island's spirit with you beyond your visit:

- Collect Souvenirs: Look for handmade crafts, artwork, or music CDs that reflect the essence of Mykonos' culture. These items can serve as tangible reminders of your experiences.

- Cooking Traditions: If you've participated in Greek cooking classes or food festivals, bring home traditional recipes to recreate a taste of Mykonos in your kitchen.

- Share Your Story: Once you return home, share your experiences with friends and family. Through stories, photos, and mementos, you can introduce them to the vibrant cultural tapestry of Mykonos.

- Keep Learning: Continue your exploration of Mykonos' culture by reading books, watching documentaries, and engaging with online resources. Deepening your understanding will allow you to appreciate your memories even more.

- Plan a Return: With so much to explore and celebrate, Mykonos' cultural scene is worth revisiting. Consider planning a return trip during a different festival or event to experience a new facet of the island's culture.

1.21 A Timeless Celebration

Mykonos' cultural celebrations and nighttime events are a testament to the island's dynamic nature and its ability to embrace the old and the new with equal enthusiasm. From ancient traditions to contemporary creativity, the island's festivals and gatherings invite you to become a part of its ever-evolving story.

As you dance, laugh, and immerse yourself in Mykonos' cultural heartbeat, remember that you're contributing to the ongoing narrative of this enchanting island. Your experiences become woven into the fabric of Mykonos, leaving an indelible mark on its cultural landscape. So, as the sun sets and the festivities begin, let yourself be swept away in the magic of Mykonos' cultural celebration.

1.22 Navigating Mykonos' Cultural Scene

To navigate Mykonos' cultural scene effectively, here are some additional tips to consider:

- Event Listings: Look for event listings in local newspapers, online travel forums, and social media groups dedicated to Mykonos. These sources often provide up-to-date information on upcoming festivals and events.

- Local Insights: Strike up conversations with locals to get insights into upcoming cultural celebrations. They might share lesser-known events that aren't widely advertised.

- Event Timing: Plan your itinerary around the dates of the festivals and events you're interested in. Some events might span multiple days, so be sure to account for that in your schedule.

- Online Resources: Explore official tourism websites, event calendars, and local cultural organizations' websites. These platforms often provide detailed information about event schedules, locations, and ticketing.

- Tickets and Reservations: For popular events, consider booking tickets or making reservations in advance. This ensures that you secure a spot and don't miss out on the festivities.

- Local Participation: Many cultural events welcome active participation from attendees. Don't hesitate to join in dances, workshops, and interactive activities to fully engage with the local culture.

1.23 A Journey Beyond the Ordinary

Mykonos' cultural celebrations offer a journey beyond the ordinary travel experience. They invite you to step into the heart of the island's identity, witness its history and creativity, and connect with its people on a profound level. Whether you're dancing to traditional rhythms, admiring contemporary art, or savoring local flavors, each moment contributes to a mosaic of memories that define your Mykonos journey.

1.24 The Power of Connection

As you immerse yourself in Mykonos' cultural scene, you're not just a spectator; you're part of a collective celebration. The power of connection is palpable as you share laughter, music, and stories with fellow attendees. These interactions bridge cultures and languages, fostering a sense of unity that transcends geographical boundaries.

1.25 Embrace the Mykonos Spirit

Ultimately, Mykonos' cultural celebrations offer a profound invitation: an invitation to embrace the Mykonos spirit in all its diversity and vibrancy. Whether you're dancing under the stars, engaging in creative workshops, or simply soaking in the atmosphere, you're participating in the island's ongoing narrative—one that celebrates its past, present, and future.

1.26 A Legacy of Memories

As your time in Mykonos draws to a close, the memories you've gathered during the cultural celebrations will remain etched in your heart. They'll serve as a legacy of your journey—a testament to the moments of joy, connection, and cultural immersion that defined your experience on this captivating island.

1.27 Carry the Culture Forward

As you return home, carry the Mykonos culture and spirit with you. Share your experiences with others, introduce them to the island's rich cultural landscape, and inspire them to embark on their journeys of discovery. Through your stories and memories, you become an ambassador of Mykonos' cultural allure, ensuring that its celebrations continue to resonate far beyond its shores.

1.28 A Final Applause

As the final notes of music fade and the last dance concludes, take a moment to applaud not just the performances but also the spirit of Mykonos itself. The island's dedication to celebrating its culture, its commitment to fostering connections, and its ability to create lasting memories make it a truly exceptional destination.

In the tapestry of Mykonos' cultural celebrations, you've woven your thread, adding to the vibrant narrative that makes this island unique. So, with a heart full of memories and a spirit uplifted by cultural connection, bid adieu to the celebrations and carry the essence of Mykonos with you as you venture forth into new horizons.

Musical Harmony: Mykonos' Music and Arts Festivals

With its sunny beaches and exciting nightlife, Mykonos is not just a refuge for partygoers but also for fans of music and the arts. Numerous music and arts events held throughout the summer bring together the island's rich cultural past with modern vitality. Create lifelong memories at the festivals in Mykonos by immersing yourself in the melodious rhythm and inventive energy on display.

Mykonos' Musical Melange: A Festival Kaleidoscope

Mykonos' music scene is as diverse as its visitors. From international DJs spinning beats that resonate across the Mediterranean to local musicians sharing the island's traditional sounds, the musical landscape here is a kaleidoscope of genres and styles. During the summer, the island comes alive with festivals that cater to various tastes, making it a melting pot of musical experiences.

1. Mykonos Music Festival: A Fusion of Global Sounds

The Mykonos Music Festival, a cornerstone of the island's cultural calendar, takes center stage each summer. Held in spectacular outdoor settings, this festival brings together artists from around the world, showcasing a diverse range of musical styles. From classical symphonies under the starry sky to contemporary jazz echoing along the coastline, this festival resonates with the island's cosmopolitan spirit.

2. Mykonos Jazz Festival: Notes That Echo Through Time

For jazz aficionados, the Mykonos Jazz Festival is a must-attend event. Set against the backdrop of the Aegean Sea, this festival celebrates the improvisational beauty of jazz music. World-renowned jazz musicians gather to create harmonies that bridge cultures and generations. Be prepared to be swept away by the soulful tunes that serenade the island during this musical celebration.

3. Mykonos Live: The Pulse of Contemporary Music

Mykonos Live, a series of events spanning the summer months, is a celebration of contemporary music in all its forms. From pop and rock to electronic and indie, this festival brings both international and local acts to the stage. Dance beneath the stars as your favorite artists perform against the backdrop of the shimmering sea. The electric atmosphere and the shared passion for music create a unique sense of camaraderie among festivalgoers.

Immerse in Art: Mykonos' Creative Expression

Mykonos isn't just a canvas of sound; it's also a canvas of artistic expression. The island's festivals extend beyond music to encompass a wide array of visual arts, allowing visitors to experience the island's creative soul.

1. Mykonos Biennale: A Visual Odyssey

The Mykonos Biennale is a celebration of contemporary visual arts. Held biennially, this event transforms the island into an open-air gallery where artists showcase their works in a myriad of mediums. From paintings and sculptures to installations and multimedia exhibits, the Mykonos Biennale is an immersive journey into the world of visual storytelling. Wander through the enchanting venues as you discover how artists interpret and interact with the island's natural beauty.

2. Art & Soul Festival: Where Art and Music Converge

Combining the realms of music and art, the Art & Soul Festival invites visitors to experience a multi-sensory extravaganza. Live music performances serve as the backdrop for exhibitions, workshops, and interactive art installations. Engage with artists as they create on the spot, channeling the island's energy into their creations. This festival is a testament to Mykonos' ability to inspire creativity in all its forms.

3. Mykonos Film Festival: Capturing Stories on Screen

Film enthusiasts find their haven in the Mykonos Film Festival. This event celebrates the art of cinema by showcasing a curated selection of international and local films. With screenings held in unique venues, such as open-air theaters overlooking the sea, the festival elevates the movie-watching experience. From thought-provoking documentaries to captivating narratives, the Mykonos Film Festival invites you to explore the world through the lens of storytelling.

A Confluence of Passion and Creativity

Mykonos' music and arts festivals are more than mere events; they're a reflection of the island's soul. As you participate in these celebrations, you become part of a narrative that intertwines passion, creativity, and the beauty of the Aegean. Whether you're swaying to the rhythms of global melodies or immersing yourself in the visual tapestry of contemporary art, Mykonos' festivals leave an indelible mark on your heart. During this vibrant energy, you'll find yourself connecting with fellow festivalgoers and artists, forming bonds that transcend borders.

Conclusion: Harmonizing with Mykonos' Festive Spirit

Section 2 of Chapter 6 invites you to harmonize with Mykonos' festive spirit through its music and arts festivals. These events showcase the island's dynamic cultural landscape, weaving together a mosaic of sounds, sights, and emotions. As you explore Mykonos' music and arts scene, you'll discover that the island's allure isn't just about its beaches and landscapes—it's also about the harmonious interplay of human expression and creativity. So, come prepared to dance, to listen, to engage, and to be moved as you become part of the symphony that is Mykonos' music and arts festivals.

Beach Parties and DJ Sets

Mykonos is well known for its exhilarating beach parties that go on until the wee hours of the morning. As the sun sets, the island becomes a wonderland of music, dance, and celebration. This section delves into the captivating world of beach parties and DJ sets that help to distinguish Mykonos as a unique nightlife destination.

The Night Comes Alive: Beach Party Magic

As twilight blankets the island, Mykonos' beaches come alive with an electric energy. The sounds of waves crashing blend seamlessly with infectious beats, setting the stage for unforgettable beach parties. The island's world-famous beach clubs and bars transform their sandy shores into dance floors that beckon both locals and visitors.

1. Paradise Beach Club: Iconic Party Playground

Paradise Beach Club stands as an emblem of Mykonos' party scene. Known for its lively atmosphere, it offers a spectrum of music styles that cater to diverse tastes. Neon lights, vibrant cocktails, and exuberant crowds create an atmosphere of pure celebration. As world-class DJs take the stage, dancers groove to the rhythm, and the energy is palpable.

2. Super Paradise Beach: All-Day Extravaganza

Super Paradise Beach is more than just a pristine shoreline; it's a destination for round-the-clock festivities. By day, soak up the sun, swim in crystalline waters, and revel in beach games. But as the sun dips below the horizon, Super Paradise transforms into a pulsating party haven. Famous DJ names grace the turntables, and the beach turns into an open-air dancefloor.

3. Psarou Beach: Luxury Meets Revelry

Psarou Beach seamlessly blends luxury with nightlife. By day, this chic beach destination offers elegant lounging experiences and exclusive beach clubs. As the sun sets, Psarou shifts gears to offer an upscale party atmosphere. A-list DJs and VIP events make Psarou a favorite among jet-setters looking to dance and celebrate in style.

4. Scorpios Mykonos: A Spiritual Dance Experience

Scorpios Mykonos transcends the typical beach party experience. Nestled in a bohemian setting, it offers a more spiritual and intimate atmosphere. With its rustic-chic décor, Scorpios draws a diverse crowd that seeks a more meaningful connection through music and dance. The sunsets here are legendary, complemented by world-class DJs who curate sets that resonate with the soul.

Musical Extravaganza: DJ Sets Under the Stars

The beating heart of Mykonos' nightlife is undoubtedly its DJ sets. Renowned international DJs and local talent converge on the island to create musical magic that echoes through the night.

1. Cavo Paradiso: A Dance Haven

Perched on a cliff overlooking the Aegean Sea, Cavo Paradiso has achieved legendary status in Mykonos' nightlife scene. Its state-of-the-art sound system, incredible views, and world-class DJs draw crowds from across the globe. The atmosphere here is electric, making it an essential stop for anyone seeking a night of unbridled dancing.

2. JackieO': Glamour Meets Music

JackieO seamlessly merges chic glamour with vibrant musical sets. Its outdoor terrace offers breathtaking views, and as the night deepens, it transforms into a dance utopia. With themed parties, drag shows, and a diverse music lineup, JackieO' creates an inclusive and lively atmosphere that invites all to join the revelry.

3. Alemagou: Bohemian Rhythms

Alemagou, located on Ftelia Beach, presents a bohemian haven for music enthusiasts. Here, the focus is on live performances, blending genres and styles into a harmonious experience. Known for its sunset sessions and unique fusion of traditional and contemporary sounds, Alemagou offers a more laid-back yet immersive nightlife experience.

4. VOID: Underground Beats

For those seeking an edgier and more underground music scene, VOID delivers. This intimate club is nestled in Mykonos Town and is known for hosting cutting-edge DJs from the electronic music scene. The industrial-chic atmosphere, combined with the latest sound technology, creates a mesmerizing audiovisual experience that resonates with the soul.

Embrace the Night: Dance Till Dawn

As you dive into Mykonos' beach parties and DJ sets, you'll discover a world where music transcends language, and the dancefloor becomes a canvas for expression. Whether you're under the stars on a pristine beach or in an intimate club surrounded by like-minded souls, Mykonos' nightlife promises an unforgettable journey through rhythm and euphoria. Prepare to dance, celebrate, and lose yourself in the pulsating heart of the island's vibrant spirit.

Creating Lasting Memories: Tips for Enjoying Beach Parties and DJ Sets

To make the most of Mykonos' electrifying nightlife, keep these tips in mind:

1. Dress the Part: Mykonos nightlife is all about glamour and expression. Don your most stylish beach attire or chic party wear to fit right in with the island's fashionable crowd.

2. Check the Lineup: Stay informed about upcoming events and DJ lineups. Many venues announce special performances in advance, allowing you to plan your nights around your favorite artists.

3. Reserve in Advance: High-demand beach clubs and parties often require reservations, especially during peak season. Secure your spot by booking ahead.

4. Arrive on Island Time: In Mykonos, the nightlife heats up later in the evening. Plan to arrive at beach parties and clubs around midnight to catch the peak of the action.

5. Stay Hydrated: Dancing the night away requires energy, so remember to stay hydrated.

Alternate between water and your favorite cocktails to keep the party going.

6. Capture the Moments: Mykonos' nightlife is as photogenic as it is lively. Capture the magical moments under the stars, surrounded by friends and music.

7. Respect the Atmosphere: While the parties are wild and exuberant, be respectful of the local culture and the environment. Keep the beaches clean and treat the island with care.

The Night Continues: After-Hours Explorations

As the DJ sets wind down and the first rays of sunlight break through, the night in Mykonos is far from over. Seek out the island's renowned after-hours spots, where the celebration continues in a more intimate setting. Enjoy a sunrise cocktail while watching the sky transform over the Aegean Sea, and revel in the camaraderie of those who share your passion for the night.

Part of the Mykonos Experience

Exploring Mykonos' beach parties and DJ sets isn't just about dancing; it's about immersing yourself in the island's vibrant soul. The convergence of music, culture, and stunning surroundings creates an atmosphere that's impossible to replicate elsewhere. From the glamour of Paradise Beach to the bohemian charm of Scorpios, Mykonos' nightlife is an integral part of the island's allure in 2023.

Whether you're dancing on the sand beneath a star-studded sky or losing yourself in the beats of a world-class DJ, Mykonos' beach parties and DJ sets are an invitation to celebrate life, music, and the shared spirit of revelry. Prepare to create memories that will resonate long after the sun has risen, carrying the essence of Mykonos' nightlife with you wherever your travels may lead.

Savoring the Sunrise: Reflect and Renew

As the music fades and the first light of dawn begins to grace the horizon, take a moment to reflect on the magical night you've just experienced. The sunrise in Mykonos is a gift to those who choose to stay up and embrace the night. Find a quiet spot on the beach, a cliffside perch, or a cozy café and watch as the sky transforms from shades of darkness to a canvas of warm hues.

This tranquil moment of solitude can be as introspective as the night was exhilarating. Allow the gentle lapping of the waves and the soft touch of the morning breeze to wash over you, bringing a sense of renewal and tranquility after the energetic night of celebration.

A Lesson in Connection and Freedom

Mykonos' beach parties and DJ sets offer more than just a night of dancing and music. They provide a unique opportunity for connection –

with fellow travelers, locals, and even with yourself. The music acts as a universal language that bridges gaps, transcends cultural boundaries, and fosters a sense of unity.

Dancing under the stars with a diverse crowd of individuals all drawn to the same rhythm reminds us of the freedom that travel offers. It's a chance to break away from the routine and expectations of daily life, embracing the spirit of adventure and the thrill of the unknown. Mykonos' nightlife serves as a reminder that life is meant to be celebrated and that every moment is an opportunity to create unforgettable memories.

Reveling in Mykonos' Nighttime Spirit

As the night turns to day and the energy of Mykonos' beach parties and DJ sets slowly fades, you'll carry with you the memories of an enchanting night filled with music, dancing, and the euphoria of celebration. Mykonos' nightlife is a reflection of the island's vibrant spirit and magnetic charm, drawing you into an unforgettable experience that becomes a part of your journey.

So, whether you're dancing beneath the stars, embracing the sunrise on the beach, or reminiscing about the beats that moved you, Mykonos' beach parties and DJ sets will remain etched in your heart as a testament to the island's ability to ignite your senses and elevate your spirit. Until your next visit to Mykonos, may the echoes of the music and the warmth of the night stay with you, inspiring you to celebrate life's joys whenever and wherever you go.

Vibrant 2023 - A Year of Mykonos Celebrations

Mykonos, which is known for its constant celebrations, is getting ready to ring in 2023 with a fervor that threatens to surpass even its illustrious previous events. It will be an especially memorable moment to enjoy Mykonos' unrivaled appeal since this year is packed with a wide variety of events and festivals that will give the island a special liveliness.

1. Mykonos' Cultural Feast: Festivals and Events

Mykonos Biennale: A Global Art Odyssey
Immerse yourself in the artistic kaleidoscope of the Mykonos Biennale. An international convergence of creatives, this event transforms the island into a living canvas. Galleries,

squares, and unexpected nooks host contemporary art exhibitions, theatrical performances, and captivating installations. It's a celebration of art's power to transcend boundaries and ignite dialogue.

Mykonos International Film Festival: Cinematic Under the Stars
For film enthusiasts, the Mykonos International Film Festival is a cinematic journey under the velvety night sky. This open-air festival showcases Greek and international films in settings that are as magical as the stories on screen. As the gentle Aegean breeze rustles through, the silver screen takes on a new allure, adding another layer to the island's cultural tapestry.

2. Musical Harmony: Mykonos' Music and Arts Festivals

Mykonos Music Festival: A Harmonious Overture

Experience the soul-stirring melodies of the Mykonos Music Festival. Against the backdrop of azure waters and quaint white buildings, world-class musicians perform classical compositions, orchestral arrangements, and contemporary pieces that resonate with the island's timeless beauty. The Aegean becomes a symphonic partner in this auditory journey.

Cavo Paradiso Festival: Electronic Rhythms on the Shoreline

Electronic music enthusiasts, prepare to be immersed in the electric atmosphere of the Cavo Paradiso Festival. Internationally acclaimed DJs converge at this iconic beachside venue, transforming it into a pulsating dance floor. With the moonlit sea as your backdrop, lose yourself in the beats of the night and the unity of dance.

3. Beachside Revelry: DJ Sets and Revelations

Beach Clubs Awaken: Dance Until Dawn

As the sun dips below the horizon, the energy of Mykonos shifts to its iconic beach clubs.

Paradise Beach Club and Scorpios Beach Club, among others, host legendary DJ sets that propel beachside revelry into the early hours. The mingling of music, moonlight, and the sound of waves creates an atmosphere of unbridled celebration.

XLSIOR Mykonos: A Celebration of Diversity and Unity
For a celebration that echoes the island's inclusivity, XLSIOR Mykonos takes center stage. A renowned gay circuit festival, XLSIOR unites a global LGBTQ+ community and allies in a jubilant celebration of love, freedom, and acceptance. Dance, music, and friendship flourish against the backdrop of Mykonos' stunning landscapes.

4. Mykonos 2023: A Year of Vibrant Celebrations

Embracing Mykonos' Unique Identity
In 2023, Mykonos is not merely hosting events—it's celebrating its own unique identity.

This year, the island honors its past, present, and future with a series of intimate gatherings, local exhibitions, and artistic showcases that capture the essence of Mykonos' allure. From traditional dance performances to insightful talks, these events showcase the island's deep connection to its heritage.

The Cultural Center: Mykonos' New Artistic Haven
This year marks the grand opening of Mykonos' new cultural center, a hub for artistic expression, workshops, and exhibitions. This center is a testament to Mykonos' commitment to nurturing creativity and fostering connections between local and international artists. It serves as a vibrant nucleus of culture, where artists and enthusiasts converge to share ideas, experiences, and visions.

Making the Most of the Celebrations: Tips and Insights

- Plan Ahead: With a rich calendar of events, plan your visit around the celebrations that resonate most with you. Check the event schedules, secure tickets in advance, and consider creating a personalized festival itinerary.

- Connect with Locals: Engage with locals to uncover hidden celebrations and smaller gatherings that might not be widely advertised. This offers a chance to experience authentic Mykonos celebrations and engage in meaningful cultural exchanges.

- Capture the Moments: Beyond attending events, take the time to capture the spirit of celebration through photography, journaling, or simply being present in the moment. These memories will become a cherished part of your Mykonos experience.

In 2023, Mykonos is poised to set new standards in celebration, uniting art, music, culture, and identity in a symphony of experiences. From artistic expressions that transcend borders to music festivals that pulse with life, Mykonos beckons travelers to partake in its effervescent energy. As you explore the island during this year of jubilation, you'll not only witness the celebrations but become an integral part of the vibrant tapestry that makes Mykonos a treasure trove of memories and connections.

Chapter 7

Unveiling the Best of Your Mykonos Journey

Accommodation Excellence: Your Perfect Retreat

Finding the right lodging is essential if you want to enjoy Mykonos' attractiveness in 2023. From opulent beachside resorts to quaint boutique hideaways, Mykonos provides a wide variety of hotel alternatives to suit different tastes. Your options will be guided by this area, guaranteeing that your stay will be nothing less than amazing.

1.1 Luxurious Beachfront Resorts: A Haven of Opulence

Mykonos is renowned for its stunning luxury resorts that provide an unparalleled blend of comfort and elegance. Set against breathtaking ocean backdrops, these resorts offer top-notch amenities, personalized service, and world-class dining. Immerse yourself in the lap of luxury at some of the island's renowned names like Belvedere Hotel and Santa Marina.

1.2 Charming Boutique Hotels: Embrace Authentic Mykonos

For a more intimate experience, boutique hotels are your ticket to embracing the island's authentic charm. These unique accommodations often feature traditional Cycladic architecture, personalized service, and a sense of local culture. Discover hidden gems like Bill & Coo Suites and Grace Mykonos for an intimate and unforgettable stay.

1.3 Villas and Private Retreats: Create Your Haven

For those seeking privacy and exclusivity, Mykonos boasts an array of stunning private villas and retreats. From panoramic views to private pools, these accommodations offer an oasis of relaxation. Enjoy the freedom to tailor your experience, whether you're traveling with a group or seeking a romantic escape.

1.4 Budget-Friendly Options: Comfort without Compromise
Mykonos caters to travelers of all budgets, and you can find comfortable yet budget-friendly options that allow you to experience the island's magic without breaking the bank. Hostels, guesthouses, and economy hotels offer cozy accommodations and a chance to connect with fellow travelers.

1.5 Insider Tips: Booking Your Dream Stay
- Advance Booking: Mykonos is a popular destination, so booking your accommodation well in advance is recommended, especially during peak seasons.
- Location Matters: Choose accommodation based on your interests. Stay near Mykonos Town for bustling nightlife or opt for a more

tranquil experience in the quieter parts of the island.
- Amenities and Facilities: Consider what amenities are important to you, such as pools, spa facilities, or proximity to the beach.
- Local Recommendations: Seek recommendations from travel forums, friends, or local experts to uncover hidden gems that may not be widely advertised.

1.6 Insider's Choice: Balancing Comfort and Adventure

Balance is the key to making the most of your Mykonos journey. Your choice of accommodation sets the tone for your entire experience. Whether you're waking up to the sound of waves crashing on the shore or indulging in the island's vibrant nightlife, your retreat should reflect your unique style. Mykonos' diverse accommodations ensure that you can find your perfect home away from home, allowing you to immerse yourself in the magic of this captivating island in 2023.

As you step into the world of Mykonos, remember that where you lay your head at night is more than just a room; it's an integral part of your Mykonos adventure. Your chosen accommodation will serve as the backdrop to the memories you'll create, ensuring that your journey is one of comfort, luxury, and authenticity. Your perfect Mykonos retreat awaits—let it be the sanctuary from which you explore the island's wonders in style.

1.7 Eclectic Accommodation Experiences: Personalizing Your Stay

Elevated Luxury Resorts: Indulge in opulence at some of Mykonos' most prestigious luxury resorts. These resorts offer a symphony of amenities, from infinity pools with panoramic sea views to lavish spa treatments that rejuvenate your senses. Experience world-class dining that showcases both local and international cuisines, creating a culinary journey within the comforts of your accommodation.

Chic Boutique Hideaways: Immerse yourself in Mykonos' distinctive character by choosing a boutique hotel. These charming establishments often blend modern comfort with Cycladic architecture, offering a unique and inviting ambiance. Relish personalized service that caters to your every need, from arranging private tours to recommending local gems off the beaten path.

Secluded Villas and Retreats: If seclusion and privacy are your priorities, consider renting a private villa or retreat. Unwind in your slice of paradise, complete with stunning views, private pools, and well-appointed amenities. Revel in the tranquility of the island as you wake up to the gentle sounds of the Aegean and bask in the serenity that only a private villa can provide.

Budget-Friendly Comfort: Exploring Mykonos on a budget doesn't mean sacrificing comfort. Budget-friendly options include cozy guesthouses, hostels, and economy hotels that offer clean and comfortable lodgings. Use your savings to immerse yourself in the island's offerings, whether that's enjoying local cuisine, embarking on excursions, or shopping for souvenirs.

1.8 Proximity to Mykonos' Charms: Choosing Your Location

- Mykonos Town (Chora): Staying in the heart of Mykonos Town immerses you in the island's vibrant energy. Wander through the iconic white-washed alleys, experience the bustling nightlife, and explore the town's numerous shops, restaurants, and cafes.
- Beachfront Bliss: If beach life is your priority, consider accommodations along the coast. Wake up to the soothing sound of waves, spend leisurely days on the sand, and enjoy easy access to beach clubs, water sports, and coastal restaurants.
- Secluded Retreats: Seek solace in the more serene parts of Mykonos, away from the crowds. Enjoy the luxury of peace, surrounded by the island's natural beauty. These areas offer a tranquil escape while still providing access to Mykonos' attractions.

1.9 Tailoring Your Experience: Prioritizing Amenities

- Relaxation and Spa: If relaxation is your goal, choose accommodations with well-equipped spas offering massages, facials, and other rejuvenating treatments.
- Adventure and Exploration: For those seeking adventure, opt for accommodations that offer guided excursions, water sports facilities, and easy access to hiking trails.
- Culinary Delights: If you're a food enthusiast, consider accommodations with renowned on-site restaurants or those located near culinary hotspots.

1.10 Insider's Wisdom: Seeking Local Recommendations

Make the most of your Mykonos experience by tapping into local insights:
- Local Experts: Reach out to local tour operators, guides, or concierges for personalized accommodation recommendations.

- Online Communities: Engage with travel forums and social media groups to gather advice from fellow travelers who have experienced Mykonos firsthand.
- Friends and Family: Ask for recommendations from those who have visited Mykonos recently. Personal anecdotes can often lead you to hidden gems.

1.11 Your Perfect Retreat: A Memorable Journey Begins

As you embark on your Mykonos journey, your chosen accommodation will shape your experience. Whether you're indulging in luxury, embracing the island's authenticity, or seeking tranquility, your retreat becomes an integral part of your memories. Every morning, it sets the tone for your adventures, and every evening, it welcomes you back with open arms. Mykonos' diverse accommodations ensure that you find a retreat that resonates with your desires and creates a backdrop for unforgettable moments. Your Mykonos journey begins the moment you step into your chosen sanctuary, making every day on the island a chapter in your personal story of discovery, comfort, and lasting memories.

1.12 Booking Strategy: Securing Your Dream Accommodation

Advance Planning: Given Mykonos' popularity, booking your accommodation well in advance is advisable, particularly if you're visiting during the high season. This ensures you have a wide range of options to choose from and can secure your preferred choice.

Flexible Dates: If your travel dates are flexible, consider planning your trip during the shoulder seasons. This not only provides a more peaceful experience but may also offer better rates and availability.

Accommodation Websites: Visit the official websites of the accommodations you're interested in. They often have exclusive offers, early bird discounts, and detailed information about amenities and services.

Online Travel Agencies: Platforms like Booking.com, Expedia, and Airbnb can offer a comprehensive list of accommodations, reviews from previous guests, and the ability to compare prices and features.

Reviews and Ratings: Prioritize accommodations with positive reviews and high ratings. These reviews provide insights into the experiences of previous guests and can help you make an informed decision.

1.13 Curating Your Mykonos Experience: Accommodation as a Catalyst

As you step into your chosen accommodation, you're not just entering a room; you're stepping into the heart of your Mykonos journey. Your retreat becomes more than a place to rest; it's a catalyst for your adventures. From the moment you wake up and take in the sunrise from your balcony to the times you return after a day of exploration, your accommodation is a sanctuary, a space that holds your memories.

Creating Memories: Picture starting your day with the tranquil sound of waves or ending it with the soft glow of the setting sun. These moments are etched in your memory, intertwining with the beauty of the island.

Personalizing Experiences: Many accommodations offer personalized services, be it arranging a romantic dinner on the beach, organizing a private island tour, or curating a spa day to unwind.

Aesthetic Ambiance: The design and ambiance of your chosen accommodation enhance your overall experience. Cycladic architecture, elegant interiors, and sea views all contribute to a sense of place and identity.

Local Insights: Your hosts or concierge can provide you with valuable insights into local experiences, suggesting lesser-known gems that aren't always mentioned in guidebooks.

1.14 The Essence of Accommodation: A Lasting Impression

As your Mykonos journey unfolds, remember that your accommodation serves as your haven—a place of comfort, rejuvenation, and inspiration. Your choice is more than a logistical decision; it's an investment in the memories you'll create, the experiences you'll have, and the stories you'll share.

A Sanctuary: After a day of exploration, your accommodation becomes a sanctuary where you can unwind, reflect, and recharge for the next adventure.

A Connection: The relationship between you and your chosen retreat becomes an integral part of your journey, fostering a unique connection to Mykonos itself.

A Constant: Amid the ever-changing landscapes and experiences, your accommodation remains a constant presence—a familiar space to return to at the end of each day.

1.15 Your Mykonos Story: A Chapter of Comfort and Adventure

As you leaf through the pages of your Mykonos journey, your chosen accommodation is a recurring theme. It's where you start and end your days, where you embark on new adventures and relive the memories created. Your accommodation choice sets the tone for your experience, defining the way you interact with the island, its people, and its offerings.

In the grand narrative of your Mykonos adventure, your accommodation is more than just a place to stay—it's a chapter in your story, a page in the book of your exploration. So, choose wisely, and let your Mykonos retreat be the canvas upon which you paint unforgettable memories, immerse in authenticity, and indulge in the island's allure. As you leave the island, your accommodation will remain an integral part of the tale you tell—a story of comfort, adventure, and the magic of Mykonos in 2023.

Mykonos on Wheels: Transportation Wisdom

On the lovely island of Mykonos, transportation is more than just a means of getting from point A to point B—it's an essential component of the experience. The different kinds of transportation that are offered will serve as your entrance to seeing Mykonos in all its splendor from the time you first set foot in this enchanted country. This section will walk you through the available modes of transportation, enabling you to get around the island with ease and create lifelong memories.

Getting Around Mykonos

1. Rental Cars and Scooters: Renting a car or a scooter is an excellent way to explore the island at your own pace. You'll find various rental agencies both at the airport and in Mykonos

Town. Keep in mind that in peak seasons, it's advisable to book in advance. A valid driver's license is necessary, and remember to follow local traffic rules.

2. Taxis: Taxis are readily available on the island, offering a convenient option for travelers. They are often stationed at popular spots like the airport, ferry terminals, and major squares. However, taxis can be in high demand during peak hours, so it's advisable to plan.

3. Public Buses: Mykonos has a reliable public bus system that connects the main areas of the island. This budget-friendly option is perfect for those looking to travel economically. Buses operate from early morning until late evening, and the routes cover the most frequented spots.

4. ATVs and Bikes: Exploring Mykonos on an all-terrain vehicle (ATV) or a bicycle can be an adventurous and enjoyable experience. ATVs are perfect for navigating rugged terrains, while

bikes are an eco-friendly way to immerse in the island's beauty.

Navigating Mykonos: Tips and Considerations

- Navigation Apps: Utilize navigation apps on your smartphone to help you find your way around the island. Google Maps and other navigation tools work well in Mykonos and can guide you to your desired destinations.

- Parking: If you're renting a car, be mindful of parking regulations. Mykonos Town, with its narrow streets, can have limited parking spaces. Utilize parking lots or designated areas to avoid any inconvenience.

- Traffic and Congestion: During peak tourist seasons, traffic congestion can be a challenge, especially in popular areas. Plan your outings accordingly, and consider starting early to avoid the crowds.

- Ferry and Water Taxis: Since Mykonos is part of the Cyclades islands, ferries and water taxis are essential for island hopping. The island's port is well-connected to nearby islands, offering you the chance to explore even more of the Greek paradise.

- Exploring Remote Areas: If you're venturing into remote or less-traveled areas, ensure you have enough fuel and provisions. Some parts of the island might not have immediate access to amenities.

Environmental Responsibility

As you explore Mykonos, remember to be mindful of the environment. Choose eco-friendly transportation options when possible, such as biking or walking shorter distances. Respect local traffic rules, avoid disturbing wildlife, and properly dispose of any waste.

Navigating Mykonos is an adventure in itself, where each mode of transportation presents unique opportunities to connect with the island's beauty. Whether you choose to cruise on an ATV, embrace the freedom of a rental car, or hop on a local bus, the journey becomes a part of your Mykonos experience. By selecting the most suitable mode of transportation for your preferences, you're not just moving from place to place; you're immersing yourself in the rhythm of Mykonos and creating memories that will forever be intertwined with the island's allure.

Cultural Etiquette and Responsible Tourism

Immersing oneself in the local culture and respecting the environment when visiting the alluring island of Mykonos is not only polite, but it also helps you leave a positive legacy for the area. This section delves into the subtle cultural subtleties of Mykonos and ethical travel practices to provide a positive experience for both tourists and residents.

Understanding Cultural Etiquette:
Mykonos, like any other destination, has its own set of cultural norms that visitors should be aware of and respect. While the island is known for its open-mindedness and welcoming attitude, keeping certain etiquettes in mind can enhance your experience:

1. Dress Respectfully: While Mykonos has a relaxed atmosphere, it's recommended to dress modestly when visiting churches, monasteries, and other religious sites. Also, consider covering up when moving away from the beaches and tourist areas.

2. Greetings: A warm "Kalimera" (Good morning) or "Kalispera" (Good evening) goes a long way in initiating conversations. Handshakes are common, and it's polite to address people by their titles.

3. Table Manners: When dining out, wait for the host to initiate the start of the meal. It's common to share dishes, so be open to trying a variety of foods. Don't forget to say "Efharisto" (Thank you) after your meal.

4. Photography Courtesy: Always seek permission before taking photos of individuals, especially in more remote or private areas. Be respectful of their privacy.

Responsible Tourism:

Mykonos' beauty is its greatest asset, and as visitors, it's our responsibility to preserve and protect it for future generations. Practicing sustainable and responsible tourism is essential to ensure that the island's allure remains intact:

1. Reduce Plastic Waste: Carry a reusable water bottle and shopping bag. Many local businesses are making efforts to reduce single-use plastic, and you can support this initiative by doing the same.

2. Respect the Environment: Stick to marked paths and trails to avoid damaging the fragile ecosystem. Adhere to "leave no trace" principles, ensuring you take your waste with you and do not disturb wildlife.

3. Support Local Economy: Opt for locally-owned accommodations, restaurants, and shops. This not only supports the community but also provides a more authentic experience.

4. Minimize Water Usage: Water is a precious resource on an island. Conserve water when possible, especially during the dry summer months.

5. Cultural Sensitivity: When engaging with locals, be respectful of their traditions and beliefs. Learn a few basic Greek phrases to show your interest in their culture, and engage in conversations with genuine curiosity.

6. Preserve Historical Sites: When visiting historical sites and landmarks, follow the rules and guidelines set by the authorities. These sites are part of the island's heritage and should be treated with care.

Creating Lasting Memories:
By embracing the cultural etiquette of Mykonos and practicing responsible tourism, you not only contribute positively to the island's sustainability but also create meaningful memories. Your interactions with locals and your commitment to preserving the environment will enhance your

journey, leaving you with a deeper appreciation for the beauty and authenticity of Mykonos.

Immersing in Local Traditions:
Mykonos boasts a rich cultural heritage that is deeply intertwined with its way of life. By immersing yourself in local traditions, you can forge a stronger connection with the island and its people:

1. Attend Local Events: If your visit aligns with local festivals or events, seize the opportunity to participate. From religious celebrations to music festivals, these events offer a window into Mykonos' vibrant culture.

2. Learn about Mythology: Delve into the fascinating stories of Greek mythology that are closely linked to the island's history. From tales of the gods to ancient heroes, Mykonos has its share of mythical narratives.

3. Visit Local Markets: Exploring local markets provides insight into the island's culinary

traditions and artisan crafts. Engage with vendors and learn about the ingredients used in traditional Greek dishes.

4. Respect Religious Sites: Mykonos is home to numerous churches and chapels. When visiting these sacred sites, maintain a respectful demeanor and avoid disrupting any ongoing ceremonies.

Creating Lasting Connections:
Responsible tourism and cultural etiquette not only contribute to the preservation of Mykonos' natural beauty but also facilitate meaningful interactions with the local community. By embracing these practices, you can create lasting connections and gain a deeper understanding of the island's essence:

1. Engage with Locals: Strike up conversations with locals to learn about their way of life, traditions, and viewpoints. These interactions often provide insights that you won't find in guidebooks.

2. Support Local Artisans: Purchase locally-made crafts and products as souvenirs. Not only do you take home unique items, but you also support the livelihoods of local artisans.

3. Volunteer Opportunities: Some organizations on the island offer volunteer opportunities related to conservation, education, and community development. Participating in such initiatives allows you to give back during your visit.

4. Learn from the Past: Mykonos has a history of resilience and adaptability. Understanding how the island has evolved over the years can provide valuable insights into its culture and character.

Leaving Your Positive Footprint:
As your Mykonos journey comes to an end, reflect on the moments of cultural exchange and the steps you've taken to be a responsible traveler. Your actions, no matter how small,

contribute to the island's preservation and the well-being of its inhabitants.

By embracing cultural etiquette and responsible tourism, you're not only ensuring that Mykonos remains a captivating destination for years to come, but you're also creating a legacy of responsible travel that future explorers can follow. As you bid farewell to Mykonos, carry the lessons learned here to your future adventures, leaving behind not only footprints but also a positive impact on the places you visit.

Capturing Memories: Photography Hotspots

Mykonos offers a variety of stunning settings that demand to be photographed, making it a visual delight for both photography aficionados and casual tourists. These photographic locations will enable you to capture the beauty and soul of Mykonos in unforgettable ways, whether you're using a professional camera or just your smartphone.

1. Chora's White-Washed Labyrinth: Immortalizing Timeless Charm

Begin your photographic exploration in the heart of Mykonos, Chora, where the narrow, winding streets are lined with dazzling white-washed buildings. Each turn presents an opportunity to capture the interplay of light and shadow on the pristine surfaces. Early mornings offer a soft, golden glow that brings out the textures of the walls, while the afternoon sun casts intriguing patterns that dance across the cobblestone streets. Experiment with different angles to showcase the intricate architectural details and the harmonious contrast of white walls against the vivid blue sky. Don't be afraid to explore deeper into the alleys; you'll discover hidden gems that provide a sense of authenticity and timelessness.

2. Iconic Windmills of Kato Myli: A Quintessential Mykonos View

No visit to Mykonos is complete without capturing the iconic windmills of Kato Myli. Perched majestically on a hill overlooking the Aegean Sea, these windmills create a silhouette that's become synonymous with the island's allure. The best times to photograph them are during the golden hours of sunrise and sunset when the warm light bathes them in a soft glow. Position yourself on the hillside to frame the windmills against the expansive sea or use them as a foreground element to enhance your composition. As the sun dips below the horizon, experiment with longer exposures to capture the dreamy, ethereal quality of this enchanting scene.

3. Little Venice's Sunset Spectacle: Colors of the Evening Sky

One of Mykonos' most romantic spots, Little Venice, offers a captivating scene as the sun bids farewell to the day. The vibrant colors of the buildings reflect in the tranquil waters, creating a symphony of hues that range from warm oranges to deep purples. The best time to photograph this scene is during the "golden hour" shortly before sunset, when the soft, diffused light enhances the atmosphere. To capture the essence of this moment, consider using a tripod to steady your camera for longer exposures, resulting in smooth reflections and vivid colors. Experiment with different angles to frame the buildings against the water and include the distant horizon for a sense of depth and scale.

4. Alefkandra Square's Twilight Glow: Elegance Under Evening Lights

As night falls over Mykonos, head to Alefkandra Square for a taste of the island's charming nightlife. The square is illuminated by the warm glow of lights, casting a magical aura over the area. Candid street photography shines here as locals and visitors gather to dine, chat, and enjoy the evening. Capture the intimacy of conversations, the joy of shared meals, and the laughter that fills the air. Experiment with different settings on your camera to capture the ambient light and the captivating ambiance of this bustling square. Consider shooting in manual mode to control your exposure and capture the details of both the illuminated surroundings and the vibrant life that unfolds within them.

5. Psarou Beach's Luxury Lifestyle: Sand, Sun, and Opulence

Switch your focus to Psarou Beach, where luxury and beauty intertwine against the backdrop of the crystalline sea. This is the ideal place to capture the essence of a Mediterranean beach vacation. The vibrant umbrellas and sunbeds juxtaposed against the azure waters create a scene that's vibrant and inviting. Play with composition by placing the colorful umbrellas in the foreground and letting the sea stretch out into the background, creating a dynamic contrast. Capture the laughter of friends enjoying the beach, the delight of children building sandcastles, and the relaxed elegance of visitors lounging in style. If you're comfortable with portraits, approach beachgoers for candid shots that showcase the carefree spirit of Mykonos.

6. Sunset at Armenistis Lighthouse: Where Sky and Sea Converge

For an awe-inspiring panoramic view that captures the magic of Mykonos at dusk, make your way to Armenistis Lighthouse. This vantage point offers a sweeping vista of the coastline, the expanse of the Aegean Sea, and the transformative hues of sunset. Arrive well before sunset to scout the best spots for composition. As the sun descends, experiment with various settings to capture the vibrant colors of the sky and the tranquil sea below. Consider using a wide-angle lens to encompass the vastness of the scene or a telephoto lens to isolate specific elements against the changing backdrop. Additionally, embrace the opportunity to capture the lighthouse itself silhouetted against the radiant hues.

7. Delos Island's Historical Marvels: Ancient Stories Preserved

Venture to Delos Island to capture more than just its natural beauty. The archaeological site is a treasure trove of history, featuring ancient ruins, statues, and mosaics that transport you back in time. Document the intricate details of the sculptures, the weathered textures of the ruins, and the narratives they embody. To capture the essence of these historical marvels, play with light and shadow to emphasize the textures and depth. Experiment with close-up shots that reveal the intricate craftsmanship and wide-angle compositions that encompass the broader context of the site. As you capture the relics of the past, you're preserving the stories that have shaped Mykonos' identity over centuries.

8. Ano Mera's Village Charms: Tranquility and Tradition

In Ano Mera, a traditional village away from the bustling tourist hubs, you'll find an abundance of opportunities to capture the authentic essence of Mykonos. The village square, surrounded by charming stone buildings and shaded by olive trees, offers a tranquil and photogenic setting. As locals go about their daily routines, you can capture candid shots that encapsulate the unhurried pace of life in Ano Mera. Focus on the details—the weathered wooden doors, the vibrant bougainvilleas spilling over whitewashed walls, and the inviting cafes that invite you to sit and observe. To enhance the feeling of authenticity, consider photographing in black and white, which can evoke a sense of timelessness that aligns with the village's traditional character.

9. Savoring Local Cuisine: Culinary Artistry Captured

Greek cuisine is an integral part of the Mykonos experience, and your camera can play a vital role in preserving these culinary memories. Whether you're indulging in fresh seafood, crisp salads, or delectable pastries, each dish is a work of art that deserves to be captured. Pay attention to the colors, textures, and presentation of the food. Get up close to capture the glistening olive oil, the vibrant hues of sun-ripened tomatoes, and the intricate layers of delicate phyllo pastry. Experiment with different angles, from overhead shots that showcase the entire spread to close-ups that reveal the mouthwatering details. Consider utilizing natural light to maintain the authenticity of the scene and avoid overpowering the dishes' natural colors.

10. Embracing Mykonos' People and Culture: Portraits of Life

The heart of Mykonos lies not only in its stunning landscapes but also in its people and vibrant culture. Engage with locals and capture candid shots that reveal the island's soul. From street vendors passionately preparing their fare to artisans crafting intricate jewelry, every interaction offers an opportunity for authentic and engaging portraits. When seeking permission for portraits, approach with respect and a warm smile. Engage in conversation, share your intentions, and be open to sharing stories. Capture the genuine expressions, laughter, and cultural connections that unfold naturally. Photograph hands at work faces full of character, and eyes that tell tales of generations. These portraits serve as windows into the lives of Mykonos' residents, transcending language barriers and encapsulating the shared humanity that unites us all.

Tips for Capturing the Perfect Shots:

- Golden Hour Magic: The golden hours of sunrise and sunset provide soft, warm light that enhances colors and textures. Plan your photography outings around these times for the most captivating results.
- Experiment with Angles: Don't hesitate to get creative with your angles. Try shooting from ground level for dramatic perspectives or from above for unique compositions.

- Leading Lines: Use pathways, streets, or shorelines to guide the viewer's gaze through the frame, adding depth and visual interest.
- Rule of Thirds: Imagine the frame divided into a grid of nine squares. Position key elements along these lines or at their intersections to create a balanced and visually pleasing composition.
- Storytelling Shots: Look for moments that tell a story. Capture interactions between people, the process of creating something, or a scene that captures the essence of a place.
- Post-Processing: While it's essential to capture an authentic scene, post-processing can enhance your images. Light editing to adjust exposure, contrast, and color can bring out the best in your photographs without compromising their authenticity.

Remember, while these photography hotspots provide a starting point, the real magic of photography lies in your perspective and creativity. Allow yourself to be inspired by the beauty and vibrancy of Mykonos, and let your camera become a tool for capturing the moments that resonate with you. Whether you're an experienced photographer or a novice with a passion for documenting memories, Mykonos' allure will undoubtedly leave an indelible mark on your images and your heart.

As you explore these photography hotspots, keep in mind that while capturing the perfect shot is a wonderful goal, equally important is being fully present in the experience. Allow yourself to soak in the ambiance, engage with locals and fellow travelers, and embrace the moments that unfold before your lens. The stories and memories you gather during your photographic journey in Mykonos will be cherished as much as the images themselves.

Conversing with Locals: Essential Greek Phrases

Connecting with the welcoming inhabitants of Mykonos is one of the most gratifying exploration experiences. Even though English is frequently spoken in tourist areas, making an effort to learn a few Greek words will greatly improve your interactions and help you become more immersed in the local way of life. Here are some crucial Greek expressions to help you communicate with people in Mykonos more effectively:

Greetings and Common Phrases:
- Γειά σας (Yia sas) - Hello
- Καλημέρα (Kalimera) - Good morning
- Καλησπέρα (Kalispera) - Good evening
- Καληνύχτα (Kalinichta) - Good night
- Ευχαριστώ (Efharisto) - Thank you
- Παρακαλώ (Parakalo) - Please/You're welcome

- Συγγνώμη (Signomi) - Excuse me/I'm sorry

Basic Communication:
- Ναι (Nai) - Yes
- Όχι (Ochi) - No
- Πόσο κοστίζει; (Poso kostizi?) - How much does it cost?
- Πού είναι; (Pou ine?) - Where is...?
- Τι κάνετε; (Ti kanete?) - How are you?
- Καλά, ευχαριστώ (Kala, efharisto) - I'm fine, thank you
- Δεν καταλαβαίνω (Den katalaveno) - I don't understand

Dining and Food:
- Μια μπύρα, παρακαλώ (Mia byra, parakalo) - One beer, please
- Ένα φλιτζάνι καφέ, παρακαλώ (Ena flitzani kafe, parakalo) - One cup of coffee, please
- Τον λογαριασμό, παρακαλώ (Ton logariasmo, parakalo) - The bill, please
- Μιλάτε αγγλικά; (Milate agglika?) - Do you speak English?

- Μιλάω λίγα ελληνικά (Milao liga ellinika) - I speak a little Greek

Navigating and Directions:
- Πώς πάω στο...; (Pos pao sto...?) - How do I get to...?
- Αριστερά (Aristera) - Left
- Δεξιά (Dexia) - Right
- Ευθεία (Eftheia) - Straight
- Πίσω (Piso) - Back
- Πάνω (Pano) - Up
- Κάτω (Kato) - Down

Engaging in Conversation:
- Τι κάνετε εδώ; (Ti kanete edo?) - What do you do here?
- Πείτε μου περισσότερα για αυτό το μέρος (Pite mou perissotera gia auto to mero) - Tell me more about this place
- Έχετε καμία πρόταση για μια εμπειρία εδώ; (Ehete kamia protasi gia mia empiria edo?) - Do you have any recommendations for an experience here?

- Πού μπορώ να βρω...; (Pou boro na vro...?) - Where can I find...?

Expressing Appreciation:
- Το αγαπώ αυτό το μέρος (To agapo auto to mero) - I love this place
- Είναι πολύ όμορφο εδώ (Ine poli omorfo edo) - It's very beautiful here
- Πέρασα υπέροχα (Perasa yperocha) - I had a wonderful time
- Είναι εκπληκτικό (Ine ekpliktiko) - It's amazing

Connecting with Locals:
Engaging with locals using even a few basic Greek phrases shows your respect for their culture and creates an authentic connection. Don't be afraid to use these phrases, and if you make a mistake, the locals will appreciate your effort and likely help you out. Learning a few Greek words is not just about communication—it's about bridging cultures and making your Mykonos journey even more memorable.

Navigating and Shopping:
- Πόσο κοστίζει αυτό; (Poso kostizi auto?) - How much does this cost?
- Μπορώ να το δοκιμάσω; (Boro na to dokimaso?) - Can I try this on?
- Έχετε αυτό σε μεγαλύτερο/μικρότερο μέγεθος; (Ehete auto se megalitero/mikrotero megethos?) - Do you have this in a larger/smaller size?
- Απλά κοιτάω, ευχαριστώ (Apla kitao, efharisto) - I'm just looking, thank you

Emergency Situations:
- Βοήθεια (Voithia) - Help
- Κλέβανε την τσάντα μου (Klevane tin tsanta mou) - Someone stole my bag
- Χρειάζομαι ιατρική βοήθεια (Hriazome iatriki voithia) - I need medical help
- Χάσαμε τον δρόμο μας (Hasame ton dromo mas) - We've lost our way

Cultural Appreciation:
- Είναι υπέροχο να μάθω περισσότερα για την κουλτούρα σας (Ine yperocho na matho perissotera gia tin koultoura sas) - It's wonderful to learn more about your culture
- Ποια είναι η ιστορία πίσω από αυτό; (Pia ine i istoria piso apo auto?) - What is the story behind this?
- Τι σημαίνει αυτό; (Ti simeni auto?) - What does this mean?

Farewells:
- Αντίο (Antio) - Goodbye
- Ελπίζω να σας ξαναδώ (Elpizo na sas xanado) - I hope to see you again
- Καλή τύχη (Kali tychi) - Good luck
- Καλό ταξίδι (Kalo taxidi) - Have a good trip

By incorporating these essential Greek phrases into your interactions, you'll find that the locals will respond with enthusiasm and appreciate your effort to embrace their language and culture. Whether you're navigating the bustling markets, sharing a meal at a taverna, or simply engaging in casual conversations, these phrases will help you build bridges and create lasting memories during your Mykonos journey in 2023. So, don't hesitate to connect with the heart of Mykonos by speaking its language and experiencing its warm hospitality firsthand.

Conclusion

As you reach the culmination of your journey through the immersive pages of the "Mykonos Travel Guide 2023," it's a moment to reflect on the profound impact that this captivating island has had on your senses, spirit, and perspective. Mykonos, a place where ancient history mingles with contemporary charm, has left an indelible mark on your heart, creating memories that will remain with you for a lifetime.

Reflecting on Your Mykonos Odyssey: A Tapestry of Memories:
Your sojourn on the island has been akin to weaving a colorful tapestry of experiences, each thread representing a unique moment that has etched itself into your consciousness. From the very first step onto the sun-kissed shores of Mykonos, you've been enveloped by its ineffable aura, a blend of authenticity, culture, and natural beauty that has enlivened your senses.

The Essence of Mykonos in 2023: Sun, Sea, and Serenity:

In the year 2023, Mykonos stood as a testament to the harmonious coexistence of nature and culture. The sun-drenched beaches, kissed by the Aegean's turquoise waves, offered not just a respite from the ordinary but an opportunity to connect with the island's soul. Whether you found yourself at the luxurious haven of Psarou, immersed in the vibrant celebrations of Paradise Beach, or reveling in the untouched beauty of Agios Sostis, Mykonos' beaches encapsulated the very essence of island life.

Beyond the Shorelines: Unveiling Delos and Ano Mera: A Journey Through Time:

Venturing beyond the sun-soaked shores, you delved into the island's rich historical fabric. Delos Island, with its ancient ruins and mythological significance, transported you back in time, allowing you to glimpse the lives of those who once walked its storied paths. Ano Mera, on the other hand, provided a contrasting narrative—a tranquil haven where traditional village life perseveres, offering insights into the island's quieter, contemplative side.

Experiences of a Lifetime: Crafting Memories in Mykonos:
Your exploration of Mykonos extended beyond the physical landscapes to include the creation of cherished memories. The island's dynamic nightlife, where music and laughter intertwine, invites you to partake in its nocturnal energy. Embarking on yachting expeditions and sailing through the cerulean Aegean waters allowed you to forge a deeper connection with the sea. Indulging in authentic Greek cuisine, be it the simplicity of a traditional taverna or the sophistication of gourmet dining, became a sensory journey of its own. Furthermore, Mykonos' shopping scene, characterized by its artisanal treasures and unique souvenirs, enabled you to take a piece of the island's essence with you.

A Year of Celebrations: Festive Moments in Mykonos:

Mykonos in 2023 was not just an island; it was a stage set for a year-long celebration of life, culture, and creativity. Festivals and events painted the island with vibrant strokes of color and sound, inviting you to join in the collective joy. The island's music and arts festivals fostered an atmosphere of creativity and camaraderie, reflecting Mykonos' dedication to nurturing both local and international talent. As the sun dipped below the horizon, the beaches of Mykonos transformed into venues of euphoria, where beach parties and DJ sets set the stage for unforgettable nights under the starlit sky.

Practical Wisdom for Future Explorations: Navigating Mykonos with Foresight:
Your journey through Mykonos wasn't solely defined by the destinations you visited; it was enriched by the practical wisdom you gained. The careful selection of accommodations, tailored to your preferences, ensured that your stay was a seamless blend of comfort and luxury. Navigating the island's transportation options allowed you to unlock its hidden corners with

ease. Embracing cultural etiquette and responsible tourism practices demonstrated your commitment to being a conscious traveler, leaving a positive impact on the places you visit. As you captured the island's beauty through your lens and engaged with locals using essential Greek phrases, you deepened your connection with Mykonos' essence.

The Farewell That Leads to New Beginnings: A Continuation of Journeys:

As you bid farewell to Mykonos in 2023, remember that your connection to this island paradise doesn't end with your departure. The memories you've cultivated, the stories you've collected, and the spirit of Mykonos will accompany you on your subsequent explorations. The allure of Mykonos transcends time and space, becoming an integral part of your journey as a traveler.

Until We Meet Again: Navigating New Horizons:

With a heart brimming with gratitude and a mind teeming with memories, you embark on your next adventure. Whether you're drawn back to Mykonos or find yourself in uncharted territories, let the lessons and experiences from this island serve as your guiding light. As you close this chapter of the Mykonos Travel Guide 2023, know that the spirit of the island remains with you, encouraging you to embrace the world with a renewed sense of wonder and a traveler's heart.

So, until the winds of destiny bring you back to Mykonos' embrace, journey forth with the knowledge that this island's magic will forever inspire you to explore, discover, and embrace the beauty that surrounds you. Safe travels, dear wanderer, and may your path be as extraordinary as the allure of Mykonos itself.

Printed in Great Britain
by Amazon